COMPANION TO THE GOOD NEWS

JOSEPH RHYMER graduated in Philosophy from Leeds University in 1952. For the next eleven years he was a member of the Community of the Resurrection; during this time he spent five years in Barbados as Vice-Principal of Codrington College. He entered the Roman Catholic Church in 1963. Since 1968 he has been Senior Lecturer in the Theology Department of Notre Dame College of Education, Liverpool. Mr Rhymer has written and edited a number of books on the Bible, and edits a national educational journal. He is deeply involved in international and inter-Church co-operation for teaching about the Bible.

ANTHONY BULLEN has, since 1964, been the Director of Religious education for the Archdiocese of Liverpool. As Director, he is responsible for the religious programme for 100,000 children in some 400 of the schools in this large Roman Catholic diocese. Father Bullen is the author of a number of books: for teachers—*Exploring God's World, Living and Believing, Growing in Christ*; and for children— *Growing Christian* (I-IV), *Twenty-Four Assemblies for Juniors*. His next book for Collins will be a discussion booklet for parents on the religious education of their children.

First published in Fontana Books, 1971
Second Impression November, 1971
Third Impression September 1972

Printed in Great Britain
Collins Clear-Type Press
London and Glasgow

Nihil obstat Lionel Swain, S.T.L., L.S.S., Censor
Imprimatur ⚜ Victor Guazzelli, Vic. Gen.
Westminster, 18th May 1971

The *Nihil obstat* and *Imprimatur* are a declaration that
a book or pamphlet is considered to be free from
doctrinal or moral error. It is not implied that those
who have granted the *Nihil obstat* and *Imprimatur* agree
with the contents, opinions or statements expressed.

COMPANION
TO THE GOOD NEWS

**JOSEPH RHYMER AND
ANTHONY BULLEN**

Collins

FONTANA BOOKS

The EASTERN MEDITERRANEAN in NEW TESTAMENT TIMES

100   0   100   200   300   400

MILES

CHARLES GREE

PREFACE

Pundits say that interest in religion is waning. If figures of church attendance can be regarded as a valid criterion, they may be right in their assumption that Christianity is the belief of a dwindling number.

It is strange therefore that the sale of Bibles is, in fact, increasing. Could it be that beneath the outward appearance of indifference many people still hanker after spiritual realities and values?

Numerous translations of the New Testament are available. The translation, *Good News for Modern Man*, first published in Fontana Books in 1968, counts its world sales in hundreds of thousands. But what of its readers? Surely they still need help to understand the Palestine of almost two thousand years ago. Without this knowledge, parts of the New Testament are bound to remain obscure.

This *Companion to the Good News* has been written for the non-specialist, the ordinary 'Christian in the pew' (or out of it) who, either on his own or with others, would like to penetrate more deeply into the gospel message.

JOSEPH RHYMER
Liverpool 23

ANTHONY BULLEN
Liverpool 3

CONTENTS

FOREWORD

Is interest in religion waning? Is Christianity the belief of a dwindling number? Figures of church attendance in Britain and other countries are taken by many to be proof of it. However, the sale of Bibles increases all the time. It suggests, I think, that beneath the outward appearance of indifference many people hunger for spiritual realities and values, and that in their minds the Bible still holds its place as the word of God.

Many translations of the New Testament are available to satisfy the spiritual hunger of English-speaking people. In my opinion *Good News for Modern Man* is the best for the general public because, besides being a complete and accurate translation, it is the one which most consistently uses today's living language of the people. Even with such a clear text as *Good News for Modern Man*, however, readers of today will need help, for example, to understand the Palestine of almost two thousand years ago. Without such knowledge parts of the New Testament are bound to remain obscure. *Companion to the Good News* has been written for the non-specialist, for the Christians in the pews and the many who are not to be found in the pews, for all who, on their own or with others, would like to penetrate more deeply into the gospel message.

The translation which this book is intended to accompany, *Good News for Modern Man,* was produced by the American Bible Society in an effort to do better what Bible Societies have always tried to do, to make the Scriptures as widely available as possible in the language of the people and at a price they can afford to pay. Within ten years, each new translation of the New Testament reaches a circulation of several million,

sometimes seven or eight million. Within four years of
its publication *Good News for Modern Man* passed the
25 million mark. In ten years this translation will
probably have been bought by 70 or 80 million people.
The figures suggest, I think, that people are learning
that there is at last a translation of the New Testament
in the true language of today. With such a translation
being used by so many people, and with such a book of
helps as this one, we will see a revitalization of
Christianity.

This book has a place in a new development. When the
Second Vatican Council issued its call for 'easy access
to the Scriptures for all' (Constitution on Divine Revelation VI, 22), it was seen that the policy coincided with
the policy of the Bible Societies and that the Bible
Societies could serve the Roman Catholic Church as
they had served the other Churches in Bible translation
and distribution. The World Catholic Federation for the
Biblical Apostolate, which came into being to help
bishops, priests and lay people in the vast pastoral work
to be done with the Bible, therefore adopted as a basic
policy that it would work wherever possible with the
Bible Societies. Now, in this book *Companion to the
Good News*, we have two Roman Catholics—one of
them, Mr Rhymer, a member of the Executive Committee
of the WCFBA—presenting a volume of helps for
readers of a translation produced by the Bible Societies.
They have done it in a way which, it seems to me, will
be perfectly acceptable not only to Roman Catholics but
to all other Christians.

WALTER M. ABBOTT, S.J.

Part I

THE BACKGROUND TO THE
NEW TESTAMENT

Chapter 1

READING THE NEW TESTAMENT

There must be few homes in Britain, the USA or Europe, which do not have a Bible. In some homes, family history is recorded on the flyleaf of the family Bible—births, marriages and deaths—and the records go back generations as the Bible is handed on down. Yet the Bible, even the New Testament part of it, fills people with mixed feelings.

Most people who have been brought up in a Christian society feel that they ought to know something about the New Testament. In one way or another it has influenced everyone, if only in the language that we speak. 'A voice crying in the wilderness'; 'a pearl of great price'; 'love thy neighbour as thyself'; 'I wash my hands of it'; 'money is the root of all evil' (an incomplete quotation, that one); 'suffer fools gladly'; and so on. The English language—and all European languages—are full of phrases from the Bible.

Slightly Odd
Yet most people would feel embarrassed if they were seen reading the Bible in public—in a bus or train—or even if their family saw them reading it at home. 'You could tell Dad knew that it was his last illness,' a friend said recently, 'he started reading the Bible.' People feel that it is only for use in real trouble, or illness, or danger, or in church. Children should be taught about it in school, but they had better not start quoting it when they leave school and start work, or when they are at home for that matter; people will think they are slightly odd if they do.

Why bother at all, then, if it is such an uncomfortable book? The answer is tied up with the most important character in the New Testament—Jesus Christ—who is just as uncomfortable to us today as he was to the people who came in contact with him nearly two thousand years ago.

Jesus Christ was born into a very ordinary, respectable, working-class family, who lived in an ordinary village in an unimportant district. In modern times, it could just as well have been a small market town in the English Midlands or the American Mid-West. 'The Messiah will not come from Galilee!' said many people of the time (John 7:41). And like so many other people who ran foul of the Roman criminal law—sometimes through no fault of their own—he was executed by the usual method reserved for people without special privileges. He was crucified.

Growing Conviction

If that had been all there was to it, Jesus of Nazareth would have been just another, insignificant human being, like most of the other people in his village. He would have faded into history as last year's leaves fade into the soil. But there was more to it than that. During his lifetime he convinced many people that he was God. He was handed over to the Romans for execution because he persisted in the claim that he was God. He came to life again, and showed even greater power than before, after being executed by experts. And very soon there were thousands of people all over the Middle East who were convinced that they were sharing in his divine power.

Down the years, that conviction has persisted and grown, as ever-increasing numbers of people have discovered the power of his divine love and proved its power in their lives. This is the heart of it all. It is not just a matter of reading about an unusually impressive teacher, or about a very brave man who was ready to die painfully rather than compromise with his principles. There is far more to it all than that. If his claims are true, Jesus Christ is the key to all our ideals and hopes, whether they are hopes for ourselves, our families, our friends, or for the whole world.

Good News

Jesus came to restore God's image in us, to complete the plan of creation, and to bring us to the place God has prepared for us from before the creation of the world. He has brought God's love into the world in all its fullness and power, and he has made it possible for us to share in it.

It is this, the love of God brought into the world and made available, that is the 'Good News' of the gospel. This is why the Gospels are printed at the beginning of the New Testament, even though they were written later than most of the other books and letters which are printed with them. They give us the Good News about Jesus Christ, the Son of God, and what he did to bring the world back to God again.

If the Gospels are so important (and they are the obvious books to start with in the New Testament), it is worth giving thought to the best way of reading them. One problem is obvious from the beginning. There are parts of the Gospels which we already know so well that we can no longer read them with fresh eyes. There are passages which we have heard and read so often—at school, in church and even in the newspapers—that we can no longer see them clearly. Passages like the 'Good Samaritan' or the 'Prodigal Son' are like pieces of over-exposed film. The camera shutter has been open too often and for too long at a time, and the picture has disappeared. We think we know these parts already, and, indeed, we may well know them by heart. So we can no longer read them with interest. The answer may be to leave them out altogether, and concentrate on the unfamiliar sections.

Through the Eyes of Others

But there is a better method than this. Jesus left nothing

in writing, so far as we can discover. Everything we know about him is at second hand. It comes to us from the impression he made on other people, the people he met and the ones he lived with. The revelations he gave about God were all written on people's hearts, not in books.

We should read the Gospels, then, through the eyes of the people who came into contact with Jesus. At first sight they seem to have led very different lives from our own. Their world passed away many centuries ago, and their simple, agricultural background was far removed from our complex society with its advanced technology and swift communications.

Yet their experiences and joys and problems were not very different from ours when you get down to what really matters in life. The father who asked Jesus to cure his epileptic child (Mark 9:14–29); or the mother who was so ambitious for her sons (Matthew 20:20–23); people like these were just as familiar with power politics, and the effects of war and international tension on the lives of ordinary people as we are. There was the same jealousy, rivalry and fear working between different districts or races as there is in our own day. Marriage, the education of children, and the opportunities for them as they grew up, meant just as much to them as they mean to us, once you have penetrated below the surface of their lives. They faced the same basic personal problems in their relationships with each other, in the family, the village, and in their jobs.

In Contact with Jesus

It was in just such circumstances as these that they came into contact with Jesus. The love that he offered them was a power that penetrated into every aspect of their lives, if they allowed it to. It transformed their lives at every point, and their relationships with each other, to make sense of it all. This is what that same love can do for us. 'Love your enemies,' said Jesus. 'You must be perfect—just as your Father in heaven is perfect' (Matthew 5:44, 48). What is more, Jesus made it possible. The Gospels show us how people reacted to Jesus when he said such things; both the people who trusted him, and the ones who thought he was a fool or worse. It is illuminating to look at him through their eyes.

Jesus is a living power. Not just through the message he taught, or through the people who have been inspired by him. His love is the power which can strengthen men's wills, and open their hearts and enlighten their minds. So there is one last point which ought to be made in these suggestions about reading the New Testament. We should ask for God's help as we approach the New Testament. He has given us the power of reason, and our reason will not let us down if we use it honestly and courageously in trying to understand him more fully.

And again, let our study of the New Testament deepen and inform our prayers. After all, it will be the obvious result if it has brought us closer to God and to the power of his love.

Chapter 2

GROUP STUDY OF THE NEW TESTAMENT

Giving and Receiving

The advantage of a group studying and discussing together a passage from Scripture is self-evident. Each member of the group brings with him his own experience, background, and level of maturity. He learns not only by listening to other members of the group, but also by giving verbal expression to his own understanding of the passage. The interplay of viewpoints almost always brings to light hidden depths of meaning which the individual may never have discovered on his own.

Moreover Christianity is of its nature social: it can never be a question of 'being alone with the Alone'. Our attempt to understand better the meaning of the Good News will be more fruitful if the search is undertaken in a spirit of readiness to give and a willingness to receive.

The Group

The optimum number for a group is about six people. More than this and the average sized living-room is uncomfortably overcrowded. A group containing more than six people would also detract from the informality of the occasion and possibly discourage shy members from contributing to the discussion.

At a time when Christians are praying and working for unity one might hope that the group is composed of members from different denominations. Whatever else their differences, Christians are united in their attitude to the Bible. Church leaders will, no doubt, continue to speak about the goal of unity, but only when it is commonplace for ordinary Christians of different denominations to talk and to pray together will a decisive step towards unity be taken.

How to Set About It

We will presume a group has been formed, and the leader for the first meeting appointed. (It is advisable to have a different leader for each session.) The group will have decided which section of the New Testament they are going to take as their theme for a series of discussions. For example, it might be the Gospel of St Luke, or one of Paul's letters, or the Sermon on the Mount, or the parables of Jesus. All should know which passage has been chosen and should read it carefully beforehand. Although the leader is not going to give a lecture, he should be acquainted with the background to the passage. The introductions to the various books of the New Testament provided in *Companion to the Good News* would be a starting point. But he might also look further afield. A number of useful commentaries are listed elsewhere (see pp. 157-8). A priest or minister from a local church would surely be willing to offer guidance.

The leader should also prepare a number of questions relevant not only to the passage chosen but also to the daily lives of the participants. These should not be examination-type questions that admit of a factually right or wrong answer. They should rather be aimed at providing the group with a stimulus to look again at the passage and to express their view on its meaning.

As an example, here are six questions for a discussion on the parable of the Prodigal Son (Luke 15:11–32).

1. How do you think the younger brother felt about his father before he went away?

2. Do the first eleven verses of Chapter 15 give any clue to the meaning of this parable?

3. Discuss carefully verse 17, 'When he came to himself'. What does this mean? What made him come to himself? In what other ways does God make sinners come to Himself?

4. What do verses 20–24 tell us about God's dealings with us?

5. Why was the elder brother angry? Are there ways

in which Church people sometimes behave like the elder brother?

6. Would the story be any the poorer if it ended at verse 24?

(These questions are taken from a pamphlet entitled *Parables for Parishes* issued by the Bible Reading Fellowship.)*

Details

The success of these discussion groups will often depend on what may seem to be unimportant details. For example, it is necessary for the meeting always to begin at the time agreed upon. If the start is delayed in order to allow for late-comers, it invariably happens that as the weeks go by, the actual starting time becomes later and later.

Similarly it is most important that the meeting should end at the time stipulated. If not, then it will almost certainly last too long. Some members of the group will want to leave but politeness will prevent them. It's best for members to go home wishing the session had lasted longer. Most groups find that an hour and a quarter is the right length.

If the meetings are held in the homes of the participants, and it's agreed that there be refreshments afterwards, it is wise to stipulate that these refreshments should be the same everywhere.

The Meeting

Obviously the meeting should begin with a prayer. The following example is no more than a suggestion:

O God, our Father, we are gathered here together in the name of your Son, Jesus Christ. He has said that where two or three are gathered together in his name, he would be with them. We believe he is with us now. May the Spirit of Jesus help us to listen to your voice

* 148, Buckingham Palace Road, London, S.W.1. This association provides excellent material for Bible study groups.

and so to discover how you want us to live. Amen.
The leader might then begin by saying something about
the place and the background of the passage to be dis-
cussed. No more than a few words are needed. Then he
reads the passage slowly aloud. The members of the
group are next given an opportunity to read it quietly
to themselves. The leader might begin the discussion by
inviting each individual in the group to say what the
passage as a whole means to him. There will inevitably
be some repetition. At times there will be digressions. If
it appears that the autobiographical experiences of the
members are leading the group into a cul-de-sac or into
a path altogether unrelated to the discussion, the leader
will gently redirect the conversation.

Tactful Leadership

Some members may be too ready to speak, others too
diffident to offer an opinion. The leader should tactfully
try to give all the members an equal opportunity to make
their contribution. To lead a discussion well requires
real skill and a skill that comes usually with practice.
For this reason it is not unusual for the first few discussions to be unsatisfactory. It takes time for the members of a group to adapt themselves to each other.

The purpose of the questions is to focus the attention of
the group on the key phrases of the passage chosen. One
aims not so much at establishing within the group a *nem.
con.* agreement. A Bible study group does not meet to
pass resolutions. Rather, each individual in the group
seeks to answer the question. 'What does God want me
to understand? What does he want to tell me tonight?'

In fact, it would be wise when the time-limit is reached
if the group were to be given the opportunity for a
moment's silence to think quietly over the answer to that
very question. One member may then be invited to make
up a prayer which, however haltingly, attempts to sum-
marize the feeling of the group after their encounter with
God's word.

Chapter 3

HOW THE NEW TESTAMENT GREW

There is a gap of nearly thirty-five years between the crucifixion and resurrection of Jesus, and the writing of the first of the four Gospels. Jesus was crucified about AD 30; Mark's Gospel was written about AD 64 or 65; Matthew and Luke wrote their Gospels some time between AD 70 and 80; John's Gospel came later still, perhaps even near the end of the first century AD.

These are long periods of time. It means that there were nearly two generations of Christians, after the crucifixion, before the first Gospel was written in the form with which we are so familiar. What was going on during this time?

The Sequence

There is broad agreement amongst scholars about the order in which the different parts of the New Testament were written, even if there is still much discussion about some of the details. Broadly speaking, this order is as follows:

AD

30	The crucifixion and resurrection of Jesus;
50	The Letter from James;
50–52	Paul's two Letters to the Thessalonians;
57	Paul's First Letter to the Corinthians, Paul's Letter to the Galatians, Paul's Second Letter to the Corinthians;
57–58	Paul's Letter to the Romans;
61–63	Paul's Letters to the Philippians, Colossians, Ephesians, and to Philemon;
64	The First Letter from Peter, Mark's Gospel;
65	Paul's First Letter to Timothy,

Paul's Letter to Titus;
75   The Letter to the Hebrews,
Matthew's Gospel,
Luke's Gospel,
The Acts of the Apostles (which was also written
by Luke, as a continuation of his Gospel),
Paul's Second Letter to Timothy;
80   The Letter from Jude,
The Second Letter from Peter;
85–95 The First, Second and Third Letters of John,
John's Gospel,
The Revelation to John.

It will be noticed that some of these, particularly Paul's
Second Letter to Timothy and the Second Letter from
Peter, are given dates after the death of the apostle who
is named as the author. These are cases where a writer
has, perhaps, applied that apostle's teaching to a later
situation, or recorded some of the apostle's teaching
which would otherwise have been lost.

The Apostles

So far as we know, Jesus left nothing in writing. All the
information about Jesus' teaching, and the things that he
did during his life on earth, comes to us from his family
and the people who met him, and lived with him. Of
these people, the most important for the formation of
the New Testament were the twelve men who had
travelled with him all through his public ministry. These
disciples or apostles lived with Jesus for three years.

After Judas hanged himself, the apostles chose another
man to be an apostle, and Peter described what his
qualifications must be:

A man must join us as a witness to the resurrection of
the Lord Jesus. He must be one of those who were in
our group during the whole time that the Lord Jesus
travelled about with us, beginning from the time John
preached his baptism until the day Jesus was taken

up from us into heaven. (*Acts 1:21–2*)

During their time with Jesus, the apostles had their lives transformed. It was not easy for them to understand Jesus, and even during the last journey to Jerusalem, they showed that they were far from prepared for the terrible suffering that would face Jesus when they arrived there (see Mark 8 : 27–33). In fact, they did not begin to understand it all until after the resurrection and ascension of Jesus. Then, under the guidance of the Holy Spirit, the facts about Jesus all fell into place, and they realized that he was truly the Son of God who had acted decisively to save the world.

The Apostles' Preaching

The apostles reached their final conclusions about Jesus in the midst of great responsibilities. They had to explain to the crowds gathered in Jerusalem who Jesus was, and what he had done. They swiftly found themselves at the centre of rapidly growing groups of people who wanted to share in the power of Jesus and the salvation that he had promised.

Some of the early sermons of the apostles are reported by Luke in Acts 2 : 14–39; 3 : 13–26; 4 : 10–12; 5 : 30–2; and 10 : 36–43. We can see in these passages how the apostles set about teaching people about Jesus. They explained that, with Jesus, the age of the Messiah and the Kingdom of God had arrived. He was the heir of David, promised by the prophets. He had opened the Kingdom of God to everyone by all the miracles and teaching he had given during his ministry. He had shown and taught that he was Son of God with power, and he had brought his work on earth to its climax in the crucifixion and resurrection. In his own body he had conquered death and opened the way to eternal life. Jesus now reigned in heaven as Messianic Lord of the universe; through the Holy Spirit he shared his power and united his people together in the Church; and he would come again in his full glory to bring the world to an end. Anyone could share in this glory by really repenting of his sins and trusting in the power and love of Jesus to save him.

How The Gospels Grew

Just to give the bare bones of the apostles' preaching like this could be very misleading. The apostles clothed these bones with information about Jesus. They drew on their experience of the years they had spent with Jesus and their vivid memories of the things he had done and said while they were with him. They described the miracles of healing they had seen, and his power over the forces of nature. They repeated the stories he had told and the teaching he had given. They showed how he looked deep into the hearts of the people he met and made them face up to themselves as they really were. Above all, the apostles described that last week in Jerusalem, culminating in the Last Supper, and the shattering experiences of Good Friday and the first Easter.

Like any good teachers, the apostles selected their material about Jesus, and arranged it carefully, to help their listeners to understand it all. They selected miracles which showed Jesus restoring damaged human faculties: withered hands, paralysed limbs, blind eyes, deaf ears and dumb tongues. Such miracles helped people to understand the new life of perfect freedom and love which they could share with Jesus. They selected parables which helped their listeners to see themselves as responsible people who must seize the opportunity to enter the Kingdom of God and respond to the love of Jesus.

The people who listened to the apostles tested their teaching in their ordinary lives and proved its truth from their own experience. They found that the Holy Spirit, who came to them when they were baptized, filled their lives with love. They all met together week after week, as Jesus had commanded, to share in the life of Jesus at the Eucharist, and to carry his life out into the world so that they could share his love with others.

While the living experience of the apostles was available, there was no need to make a written record of their witness to Jesus. But as the apostles were executed or grew old, it became important to preserve what they had said and the way in which they had said it. And so the Gospels came to be written. They had grown into the form in which we now have them over many years. They enshrine the impression made on the apostles by Jesus, and the living experience of those first generations of Christians as they discovered the power of Jesus transforming their lives.

The Letters
We have windows into the lives of those first Christians through the letters which they wrote to each other. These letters are all the more valuable because they arose from the many different problems and situations that the early Christians had to face. They were written by the men who shouldered the deep responsibility of helping the new Christians in cities throughout the Near East. Human nature has changed very little down the centuries, and we can learn much from those early Christians as they struggled to show the love of Jesus in their relationships with each other and with the other people in their cities.

More important still, we can understand the Gospels so much more easily if we read them with the help of the Letters. For the Gospels present us with the picture of Jesus which made sense to those early Christians and transformed their lives.

The following five chapters are most important for an understanding of the New Testament. In many ways the world of the first believers in Jesus was entirely different from our own. It is true that human nature does not change: men and women then, as now, were liable to the fears and aspirations, virtues and vices, joys and sorrows common to all humanity of whatever age.

But the way the first converts to Christianity lived their lives, their attitudes to society, to authority, to religion, were all deeply rooted in the cultures and nationalities proper to their time.

The gospel preached by Jesus and afterwards by his first followers took into account the diverse human situation in which men of that time lived—a situation vastly different from our own. If we are to penetrate the gospel message we must, to some extent, see and hear this message with the eyes and ears and outlook of the first-century Christian.

These first Christians were Jews, Greeks and Romans. Some shared in the culture and outlook of all three ethnic groups. For example, Paul was a Jew who spoke and thought mainly in Greek and was at the same time proud of his Roman citizenship. In the following three chapters we attempt to give a pen portrait of what it meant to be a Roman, a Greek and a Jew at the time of Christ. In chapters 7 and 8 we describe a fictitious character, Alexander, a prospective convert to 'the Way' who, it is plausible to suppose, was typical of thousands who asked to be admitted into the family of God's new people.

Chapter 4

THROUGH ROMAN EYES

The Power of Rome
At the time of Jesus, the ancient world of Europe and the parts of Asia and Africa that bordered the Mediterranean Sea were dominated by the Romans. Whatever their attitude might be, the people who lived at that time were organized and controlled by the Roman power. Some groups hated Romans and fought them, openly or secretly; others welcomed them and became rich and powerful from the opportunities of trade, and collaboration in the administration of the Empire. Most of the ordinary people just accepted them as an inevitable part of the everyday scene.

By the time Jesus had grown to manhood, Palestine had already been part of a Roman province for nearly a hundred years, and most of the Mediterranean world had been under Roman control for considerably longer than that. The Roman power reached deeply into everyone's life. At the end of the Sermon on the Mount, when Jesus returned to the small port of Capernaum on the Sea of Galilee, the first person he met was the centurion in charge of the local Roman garrison (Matthew 8:5). He would be as familiar a figure as a policeman is in modern times.

The Evidence of Rome
The signs of the Roman presence could be seen and felt everywhere. In the cities and towns there would be at least some buildings whose architecture reflected the orderliness and confidence of the Roman administrators. In the larger cities spacious baths and elegant temples opened from wide streets designed as much for ceremonial processions as for traffic. Even in Jerusalem the

Temple itself was overlooked by the great guard tower manned by Roman soldiers (see Acts 21:30–40).

In the countryside throughout the Empire, the magnificent paved roads were eloquent testimony of Rome's control, and the remains of camps and staging posts for the legionaries and imperial couriers show how the traffic on the roads was dominated by the swift movement of troops and officials. More ominously, all too frequently the traveller would be likely to pass crosses on the outskirts of a town or village, with a condemned criminal slowly suffering the cruel death which Roman law required for people who could not claim special privileges.

Local administration was normally left in the hands of native magistrates or puppet kings (such as the Herods), if they proved that they were loyal to Rome. But everyone felt the burden of Roman taxation, in addition to local taxation. These Roman taxes were collected by private businessmen (the 'publicans' in the Gospels) who paid for the privilege and made a handsome profit from it.

Status and Privilege

The general description 'Roman' covered a very wide variety of people. In the earlier period, before New Testament times, Rome was controlled by the aristocratic families who ruled through the Senate and filled the senior administrative positions. The ordinary citizens had considerable power through their general assembly, but the bulk of the manual work was carried out by slaves, who formed the major part of the population. Slaves remained the basis of the whole Roman economy throughout the time of the Empire, and although some rose to positions of influence, most slaves were entirely at the mercy of their owners. Onesimus (see the Letter to Philemon) was lucky to have a master who would treat him with compassion.

By New Testament times, power was firmly in the hands of the emperor, and the rank of 'Roman citizen', with its valuable status and privileges, was enjoyed by many people in all parts of the Roman world. They received this by birth, by performing some service for the state, and even by purchase (see Acts 22:25–9).

The Ambitions of a Roman

Without doubt, the government service offered the greatest opportunities of comfort, security and power to a Roman, particularly service in the emperor's household. The problem of administering so vast and complex an empire was solved by delegating large powers to subordinate officials. A young man who was fortunate enough to be born into the senator class would work his way up through a series of administrative positions, which could finally see him in sole charge of a rich and important province of the Empire.

On the way he would have held civil and military posts which involved administering the law as a magistrate, organizing the trade and taxation of a whole district, and commanding the security forces. The Roman legions were the final weapon to enforce an official's authority, just as they were the essential guardians of the frontiers with the barbarians and the protectors of the famous Roman peace. Within his district, or his command, such a man had almost unlimited authority and he expected absolute obedience. In practice, he was sensitive to local feeling, and a Roman citizen could always appeal to the emperor himself against the legal decisions of any official (see Acts 25:1–12).

The lower ranks of the army, and of the administration, offered wide opportunity for freemen to rise to positions of real responsibility and influence, particularly as the higher administrators and officials often remained only for a short time in any one position. Centurions, who had risen through the ranks until they had charge of a section of a legion, were the backbone of the Roman army, and were often given independent command of a small garrison. They were widely travelled men, and it is interesting that every centurion mentioned in the New Testament is shown as a compassionate and honest person (see Matthew 8:5–13; Luke 23:47; Acts 10:1–48; 23:16–18). Such men sometimes joined in the worship at the Jewish synagogues, and it is clear that many of these Romans of lower rank were attracted to Christianity as soon as it began to spread through the Empire.

The Roman Religion

The Roman state and the Roman way of life made a deep impression on the men who served it. Loyalty, and obedience to the state in the person of the emperor, were the virtues most admired. When the centurion of Capernaum wanted to show that he recognized the authority and religious power of Jesus, he did it by comparing it with the authority which he himself had from the emperor (Matthew 8:5–13).

The religious cult of worshipping the Roman emperor had already begun in New Testament times, but it was combined with the worship of the City of Rome as a god. The Roman community was the real god of the Romans, no matter how many other gods they might worship; the emperors were worshipped as the symbols of Rome and the heads of the Roman community. The great estates, with their ordered employment of an army of slaves, were as much expressions of the Roman genius as were the army and the law-courts, and this genius was the true basis of Roman religious feelings.

Yet, at the same time, superstition played an extraordinary part in people's lives. The entrails of sacrificed animals and such natural events as the flights of birds were interpreted by priests and soothsayers as essential guides for decisions. The average Roman was convinced that the stars controlled his life in some way, so astrology was taken so seriously that it could delay or otherwise affect important government decisions.

As the Empire expanded into Asia, new religions began to attract the Romans, particularly the ones who had seen military service in the East. Many of these religions were 'mystery' cults, with secret rites and 'knowledge' which gave the worshippers hope for a future life and release from suffering. The old gods, whom the Romans shared with the Greeks, held out little hope for any real life after death. The new cults did much to satisfy this need, and also helped to break down barriers of race and caste by treating all the initiates as equals.

But the most influential beliefs amongst educated Romans came from the Greek philosophers. Stoicism was particularly attractive, for it taught that the world is controlled by a supreme and benevolent god, and men are free to cooperate with the harmony that this supreme power produces in nature. The Stoics believed that misfortune or suffering cannot harm the man who directs his will towards this harmony, for he will have control over all his desires and need not be troubled by anything done to him from outside. In the end it was a cold and selfish belief, but it helped men to live in a world full of human cruelty and of natural forces beyond human control.

Perhaps this helps us to understand such a man as Pontius Pilate as he struggled with the problems of administering the district of Judea. To us, he seems to be a strange mixture of tolerance and ruthlessness, fear and indifference; but he acted swiftly when Jesus was presented as a threat to the power and authority of the Roman emperor (see John 19:4–16).

Chapter 5

THROUGH THE EYES OF A GREEK

The whole of the New Testament, from the Gospels to the Book of Revelation, was written in Greek. This simple fact tells us a lot about the Greek influence in the ancient world of the Near East. Although the Romans had imposed their rule over the entire area by the time Jesus was born, Greek was the most widely spoken language, and the Greek way of life spread far beyond the mainland and islands of Greece. Even the Old Testament had been translated into Greek nearly a hundred and fifty years before the birth of Jesus, because so many of the Jews spoke Greek rather than Hebrew or Aramaic.

Alexander the Great, who conquered so much of eastern Europe and the Middle East more than three centuries before Jesus, had helped the remarkable spread of Greek civilization. Wherever he went, he founded elegant Greek cities, each with its temples, amphitheatre, gymnasium and open market-place. These public buildings encouraged discussions and the exchange of ideas, as much as they served the needs of worship, drama, athletics or trade. Philosophers, scholars and teachers travelled from city to city, and could be sure of a hearing. Great cities, such as Alexandria in Egypt, became centres of learning and scholarship which survived long after Alexander's empire had collapsed.

It was an inheritance of past glories that strongly influenced many of the Roman emperors, particularly Augustus (who was emperor at the time when Jesus was born), Nero, Vespasian (who ruled in the middle of the first century AD, during the time when the Gospels were written), and Hadrian. Under such rulers, the fashion for the Greek way of life received strong encouragement.

The Problems of Life

The relentless quest for knowledge, and for answers to the fundamental problems of life, can be traced back to the Greek colonies in Asia Minor six centuries before the beginnings of Christianity. The first philosophers tried to discover the universal laws which govern nature and human behaviour, and although their conclusions often seem strange, they made genuine attempts to test them by scientific experiments. They believed that human reason could unlock the secrets of the universe. Men such as Pythagoras, who lived about 530 BC, laid the foundations of pure mathematics, and in 300 BC Euclid of Alexandria wrote the geometry book which remained the standard school text-book until the end of the nineteenth century.

Ruthless Questioning

The most influential of the Greek philosophers were the men who turned to the study of human nature and the ideals that people try to express in their lives. Socrates marked the start of a succession of great philosophers who tried to discover universal truths that all men could recognize. They believed that ignorance was the main cause of the world's unhappiness. If only they could discover the true definitions of goodness, beauty and justice, and show others how to discover them, they would be able to recognize them in every kind of human situation. Then they would know how to shape their lives to achieve real satisfaction. Socrates taught that such knowledge could only be obtained by ruthless questioning of human opinion, no matter how great was the authority which taught it, until truths were discovered which survived all attempts to disprove them.

Many people were antagonized by Socrates' methods of argument, for it made them look foolish and ignorant. In 399 BC the Athenian authorities executed Socrates for corrupting his pupils and attacking traditional religious beliefs, but his influence grew stronger after his death through the people who had listened to him.

Longing for Perfection

The most famous of these was Plato, who recorded the kind of discussions that Socrates had led. Plato went on to develop his own philosophy of a changeless, eternal and ideal world which is the model for the imperfect and unsatisfactory world in which men live. Every man, taught Plato, has a longing for the perfection which he dimly knows is there, and it can be reached if human reason is used properly. Then all human problems could be solved, and mankind would live in perfect harmony.

Plato, in his turn, taught Aristotle, who laid the foundations of logic and made a remarkable synthesis of scientific knowledge of his time. Such men were deeply immersed in politics, and tried to influence the rulers of their time to produce states modelled on their philosophies. For a time, Aristotle was tutor to the young Alexander the Great, but he would hardly have approved of the methods by which Alexander conquered so much of the known world.

Although they had little success in their attempts to create an ideal human society, the philosophers wakened men to the power of human reason. They examined the world in which they lived with critical eyes, even if they could do little to change it. The Greeks were fascinated by the mysteries of the universe and of human nature, and they longed to find the truth. It was a fascination and a longing which would find deep satisfaction in the Christian gospel.

Gods and Goddesses

The Greek people were proud of the great authors who belonged to their nation: poets, dramatists and historians, as well as philosophers. But it was the popular Greek religion which left the deepest impression on the lives of most of the Greek people, and its influence was felt throughout the Mediterranean world.

A city such as Corinth, the great port in the southern part of the Greek mainland, possessed temples dedicated to a wide range of gods and goddesses, from tiny street shrines to the great buildings where Apollo, Asclepius, Aphrodite, Poseidon and Athena were worshipped. Mankind is surrounded by natural forces which have profound effects on people's lives, but men have very little control over them. The people thought that gods controlled the mysterious forces shown in the growth of crops, the fertility of animals, the weather, the fortunes of war and all the uncertainties of life in the ancient world. Every aspect of life had its god or goddess, each with its appropriate worship, temples, priesthood and regular feasts.

Goddess of Love

Astrology, which holds that the movements of the stars and planets influence events on earth, was taken seriously at every level of society, and this overlapped into divination. The future was confidently predicted through horoscopes, dreams, the flight of birds, the weather, and the entrails of sacrificed animals. In general, it was superstition raised to the level of religion, and it shows how far the average man's life was dominated by fear and insecurity.

Sacred prostitution played a large part in popular religion, where Aphrodite was worshipped throughout the Greek world. She was primarily the goddess of love, beauty and fertility, but she was also worshipped as goddess of the sea and the protector of seafarers. The temple of Aphrodite at Corinth had a thousand prostitutes on its staff, and this must have been the religion of many of the Christians of Corinth before they were converted by Paul (see p. 120). It helps us to understand, perhaps, the passages of the New Testament that forbad women to take an active part in Christian worship (see 1 Corinthians 11:2–16; 14:34–5).

Influence of Ideas

Roughly half of the population of Greece were slaves, by birth, capture in war, or in payment of debts, and such people were trained or educated only if their masters saw profit in it. But the children of free citizens had an elaborate and thorough education available for them, often provided at the expense of the State. The content of studies ranged from military skills to religious and moral ideas. From the age of six, when a boy went to the elementary school, to twenty, when he was considered a fully formed citizen, the youth passed from the rudiments of reading and arithmetic through a thorough study of literature and a rigorous athletic training before completing two years of military service.

Greek literature, in philosophy, poetry and drama, grew out of the natural life of the people, for every Greek city of any importance had its theatre. Many of these theatres were large enough to hold several thousand people. The religious festivals were occasions for athletics and plays which were held in honour of the gods. The great festivals held every four years at Olympia, the main Greek sanctuary of Zeus, lasted five days, in which the first and last day were given to sacrifices and the other days to the great athletics competitions.

The Greeks were never sufficiently united to build a lasting empire or impose their rule on the ancient world, but they conquered the world in a more subtle way through their religion, their culture and their general attitude to life. When the Hebrew people rejected the new Christian religion which started amongst them, it was not surprising that Christianity grew so strongly on Greek soil. It appealed to so much that the Greeks longed for, and gave them access to a power which gave security and meaning to the world in which they lived.

Chapter 6

THROUGH THE EYES OF A JEW

By the time of the New Testament, the Hebrew people had known only three short periods of freedom in the course of thirteen hundred years or more. The seventy years of rule by David and Solomon, after the defeat of the Philistines in 1000 BC, gave them their first experience of real security; there were seventeen years of freedom from 625 to 608 BC, and they were free from 142 to 63 BC. When Jesus was crucified by the order of a Roman official, the Romans had controlled Palestine for nearly a hundred years. In AD 70, forty years after the crucifixion, the Romans destroyed Jerusalem after a Jewish revolt, and the Hebrew people lost their national State until its restoration in our own times.

The Heart of the Matter
It was amazing that the Hebrews retained any sense of national identity under such a history of strain and foreign occupation. The main reason must be found in the Hebrew religion. And at the heart of the Hebrew religion was the unshakable conviction that Yahweh, the Hebrew God, had rescued the people from slavery in Egypt more than twelve hundred years before the birth of Jesus, and had made a special covenant with them.

From this beginning there had grown the belief that Yahweh was the only God, the supreme power who had made the entire universe and sustained it in every detail of its existence. But he was far from being a God of naked power. At the Exodus, the escape from Egypt, he had shown that he valued every single person, and that he expected each of them to recognize this value in each other. The Hebrews rooted all their laws in this experience. The love, justice, and respect which the law re-

quired each man to show towards his neighbour came
from the God whom they worshipped. If they betrayed
these principles in their dealings with each other, they
were breaking the covenant which God had made with
them.

True Freedom

All their worship centred on the Exodus and the Covenant. Their main festivals were harvest feasts, held to
celebrate their joy and gratitude as each of the main
crops was safely gathered in the course of the agricultural
year. But in the power which produced the crops they
recognized the same power which had brought them
safely out of Egypt and settled them in Palestine. The
first of the three great festivals of the year, the feast of
Unleavened Bread, began with the Passover. The blood
of the Passover lambs, sacrificed by each Hebrew family,
symbolized the holy power which had protected them
from death in Egypt and redeemed them. The Passover
meal expressed the privileged fellowship created during
that journey from death to life and freedom. The ever-
renewed memory of the Exodus convinced the Hebrews
that they were truly free, even when foreign soldiers were
garrisoned throughout their country, and foreigners grew
rich on the taxes they exacted.

Peace and Prosperity

With such a conviction of the power of God, the Hebrews naturally looked forward to a time when they
would be politically free again, and supreme amongst
the nations of the world. It would be a supremacy which
would bring peace and prosperity not only to the Hebrews themselves, but to all other nations as well. The
rest of the world would recognize the goodness, the
power and the authority of God, and choose to worship
him. Then love and peace would spread throughout the
world, and the whole universe would become perfect, as
God intended it to be when he made it.

The Messiah would be the architect, the builder and the victor who would make this dream come true. David was the model for the leader who would defeat the Hebrews' enemies and bring in an age of universal peace. For David had defeated the Philistines and given the nation its first real experience of security. He had established Jerusalem as the national capital, and he had brought the sacred Ark of the Covenant there to show that the nation lived by the power of God. David's rule had been confirmed by a special covenant (see 2 Samuel 7), and he had accepted the rebuke of God's prophet and ruled in God's name after the terrible crime in which Uriah was murdered.

Age of Glory

'Messiah' means 'anointed'. It referred to the Hebrew practice of conferring authority on kings and priests by anointing them with consecrated oil. They then shared in the power of God, so that they could carry out their duties as officers of the Covenant. The Messiah would show this power, and bring in a new covenant, more perfectly than any leader before him. He would be perfect king and perfect priest, ruling the people in God's name and sharing the full power of God's love with them. Then the Hebrews who had remained faithful to the Law of God would share in the glory of the new Kingdom of God as it spread throughout the world.

The Old Testament Points the Way to the New

There are many prophecies in the Old Testament that speak of this Messiah and the age of glory which he would bring in. Isaiah 9 and 11 contain the most famous predictions, but a devout Hebrew at the time of Jesus treasured other passages as well. God's covenant with David pointed forward to the Messianic age and the coming of the Son of Man in Daniel 7:21–6. Zechariah 9:9–10 describes the triumphal entry of the Messiah into Jerusalem, and Jeremiah 30–1 gives a picture of the return of all the Hebrews from their places of exile to form a new people of God. Some passages suggest that the Messiah will only triumph after he has endured great suffering (see Isaiah 42:1–9; 49:1–6; 50:4–11; 52:13–53:12), but the main impression is one of effortless triumph in which the Hebrews will have revenge over their enemies.

Jerusalem and the Temple

For a thousand years, from Solomon to the time of the Roman emperor, Vespasian, the Temple was the chief glory of Jerusalem. Solomon had built the first Temple, to house the Ark of the Covenant. When Jesus was born, a new Temple was being built in Jerusalem, and it was not completed in all its magnificence until twenty-four years after the crucifixion. It was the most important place in the world for a Hebrew, for it was the only place where sacrifices could be offered. Every Hebrew tried to make the pilgrimage to the Temple in Jerusalem for the great festivals, no matter how far away he lived. Six years after it was completed, it was destroyed in the bitter fighting against the Romans which ended the Jewish war of AD 67–70, and it has never been rebuilt. The Wailing Wall in Jerusalem is part of the foundations of the Temple. If the Temple can still move people so deeply in our own times, it can be imagined how much it meant to an ancient Hebrew.

The psalms were the hymn book of the Temple and the chief way in which the people shared in the worship at the Temple sacrifices. Many of the psalms contain references to the Temple (e.g. Psalms 5, 11, 18, 27, 29, 48, 65, 68, 79 and 138), and many more refer to the city of Jerusalem, or Zion, as it is sometimes called (e.g. Psalms 2, 9, 14, 20, 48, 50, 51, 68, 69, 74, 76, 78, 79, etc.). The deepest hopes of the ordinary Hebrew people are enshrined in the psalms, for whoever wrote them, they have survived because so many ordinary Hebrew people used them as their prayers. They cover the whole range of human feelings, from love to hate, from thanksgiving to deep complaint, from songs of triumph to cries for help and protection.

Some of the psalms (particularly Psalm 118) expressed the people's hope for the Messiah, the saviour sent from God.

A Scattered People

Far more Hebrews lived outside Palestine than within its borders. Indeed, a really typical Hebrew in New Testament times was far more likely to live in Rome or Alexandria than in Jerusalem. From the time when the Babylonians deported the Hebrews to Mesopotamia in 587 BC, the Hebrews had been a scattered people. Their loyalty to Jerusalem, their faith in the God of the Covenant, and their obedience to Hebrew Law, all helped them to preserve their identity. The Hebrew scriptures (the 'Old Testament') had long been translated into other languages (most frequently Greek) to meet the needs of the scattered people.

Sacrifice was forbidden outside Jerusalem, but the Hebrew communities gathered together on the Sabbath each week for scripture studies, prayer and discussion. These *synagogues* (from the Greek, meaning 'to gather together') were also the schools in which the young Hebrews were educated, and the places where a Hebrew traveller could be sure of finding fellow countrymen. In many cities, Hebrews formed a significant part of the population, with a distinct district of their own. But Jerusalem remained the centre for all the scattered people, and they supported the Temple with gifts and special taxes.

Typical Hebrews

The apostles were typical Hebrews. Jesus drew them from his own home district, the area bordering on the Sea of Galilee, sixty miles north of Jerusalem. Even though some of them were young, they were adult Hebrews with clear ideas about their religion, and a deep devotion to it. When Jesus spoke to them about the Messiah or the Covenant, about sacrifices and the Kingdom of God, they thought as Hebrews as they listened to him. They accompanied him on pilgrimage to Jerusalem and ate the Passover with him on the night before he was crucified. All the time, Jesus was educating them and preparing them for their responsibilities. It helps us to understand them and their message about Jesus if we remember that they were Hebrews before they were Christians.

Chapter 7

ALEXANDER THE CONVERT

What would a citizen of the first century AD have found when he made contact with the local Christian group? Let us look at those early Christians through the eyes of Alexander, a citizen of Colossae in Asia Minor. He would have been, perhaps, a merchant in the textile industry which gave Colossae its prosperity. Perhaps he arranged for the cloth to be transported to the port of Ephesus, 110 miles away on the coast of the Aegean Sea, where it would be shipped across to Greece, to Italy, to Caesarea in Palestine, or down to Egyptian Alexandria.

But whatever his trade or position, he met with the same kind of reception from the Christians. In his own social and commercial world, rank, birth and status surrounded Alexander in everything he did. But to the Christians all men were equally in need, and all were equal before God. The privileged citizen of Rome, the ordinary freeman and the slave; the governor of a province or the beggar at the city gate; all were caught in the general helplessness of the human situation. All men were separated from God by sin—their own sin and the sin of others—and they were helpless unless they accepted the help of Jesus Christ, the crucified Jew who had risen from the dead.

The Christians told Alexander that they could set him on the way to a new life, he could become a new man, transformed by the love of God:

This is the new man which God, its creator, is constantly renewing in his own image, to bring you to a full knowledge of himself. As a result, there are no Gentiles and Jews, circumcised and uncircumcised, barbarians, savages, slaves, or free men, but Christ is all, Christ is in all! (*Colossians 3:10–11*)

A Sponsor

Sixty years after the crucifixion, the first serious persecution of Christians started under the Roman emperor, Domitian. John, the Bishop of Colossae and all that part of Asia Minor, was exiled to the island of Patmos, which the Romans used as a prison. In any case, the Christians were cautious before they admitted a stranger to their meetings.

Sponsored by someone who knew him, Alexander was invited to one of the weekly meetings of the Christian community. These were usually held late on a Saturday night and went on until the early hours of Sunday morning, or even until daybreak. There were no 'free weekends' in the ancient world, except amongst Jews who kept the Saturday Sabbath; there were only the breaks provided by the many pagan festivals. Christians ignored the pagan festivals, but they met to celebrate the resurrection of Jesus on Sundays. For most Christians this had to be fitted into the night, between two days of work.

A Christian Meeting

The Christian meetings were far more than church services in the way that we know them. In some places there may have been church buildings, but in Colossae the church may still have been meeting in Philemon's house, as it was when Paul wrote his letter. Everyone brought food, to be pooled and shared. Then there were church matters to attend to, such as making provision for the poor, and hearing news and letters from other Christian groups.

One of the group had been appointed 'presbyter', by John—the *episkopos* ('overseer' or 'bishop') of the area —and he would preside over the meeting if the bishop could not be there. The title of 'priest' was later given to such a man. Other men in the group had been appointed to be 'deacons', literally 'those who serve at table', to help with the administration of the local church. And there were others whose special gifts for teaching, or healing, had been recognized officially.

As the meeting went on, it turned to the discussion of problems which the members of the church were having to face in their lives. The teaching of Jesus was brought to bear on the questions, to work out solutions for the special local circumstances in Colossae. If the bishop was present, he would certainly lead this discussion and sum it up with an exposition of the Church's teaching on the matter. By this time, more than fifty years after the crucifixion and resurrection, the Church had accumulated a very large amount of experience about the Christian way of life. The Christians in Colossae could draw on this experience, through John their bishop, for he was in constant touch with the other leaders of the Church.

The Scriptures

Sixty years after the crucifixion, at least three of the Gospels had been written (Mark, Matthew and Luke) and perhaps John's Gospel also. The local church would have a treasured copy of one of them, and copies of some of the letters which the apostles had written to various local churches. To these early Christians, 'Scripture' meant the Old Testament, which recorded the long years of discovery when God was revealing himself to the Hebrew people. The promises and insights of the Old Testament had been fulfilled in Jesus, so the Christians turned to the Old Testament to help them to understand the saving power that was at work amongst them.

The scriptures of the Old Testament, and the Gospels and letters which were forming the New Testament, were read at the weekly meetings, and their meaning and significance would be explained. All this was interspersed with hymns and with prayers. One of the first Christian hymns is quoted by Paul in his Letter to the Philippians (2 : 6–11)—we sing it nowadays as 'At the name of Jesus, every knee shall bow'. Alexander, a newcomer to the

Christian meeting, would find that most of the hymns used were the psalms of the old Hebrew religion, which are in the Old Testament, translated into Greek.

One of the deacons led the prayers, even though several of the people present had contributed to them spontaneously, and the deacon then summed up all the prayers in a 'collect' which collected the prayers into one simple expression. This part of the meeting ended, probably, with a long litany of intercession and thanksgiving, led by a deacon with all the people repeating a simple response throughout it.

The Eucharist

By now the night was well advanced, and the sense of unity would be growing towards a climax. At this point, Alexander—and everyone else who was not a full member of the Christian Church—would be asked to leave. The climax of the meeting was only for the fully committed, who had been fully instructed into the Church's teaching, and had accepted it and been baptized.

The people who remained gathered round the bishop, or the presbyter, and presented him, through the deacons, with a single large loaf, and with wine and water. Then they began the most solemn part of their meeting, in which they prepared to renew their share in the sacrifice of Jesus, and the life which he had shed so that it could be shared by all. The outward action was simple. Following the pattern which Jesus had established at the Last Supper, the priest took the bread and wine, blessed it, and distributed it to the people. The bread was broken in small pieces from the loaf, and the wine was given in a single large cup.

This simple ceremony was accompanied by a great prayer of thanksgiving. This prayer connected it all with the long series of wonderful actions in which God had shown his love in the world, and which reached their climax in the crucifixion and resurrection of Jesus. The words of Jesus at the Last Supper were repeated over the bread and wine: 'This is my body, which is for you. Do this in memory of me. This cup is God's new covenant, sealed with my blood. Whenever you drink it, do it in memory of me.' (I Corinthians 11:24–5.)

Then, with a brief prayer and another hymn, the meeting ended as dawn broke. The people might well be going out to hostility from neighbours and civic authorities. The ordinary worries of everyday family life could well have been magnified by poverty, for officials and civil servants and many others would lose their jobs if, as Christians, they cut themselves off from the religious life of a pagan city. But their share in the glory of Christ meant sharing in his sufferings as well, and their faith bound them all together with links stronger than any merely human fellowship.

Chapter 8

ALEXANDER IS BAPTIZED

Whatever a person's background may have been, there was much for him to learn before he could be received as a full member of the Christian community. Accepting Christianity meant accepting a whole new way of life and looking at the world from a new point of view. And at the heart of it there is the startling mystery of the cross:

> We proclaim Christ on the cross, a message that is offensive to the Jews and nonsense to the Gentiles; but for those whom God has called, both Jews and Gentiles, this message is Christ, who is the power of God and the wisdom of God. For what seems to be God's foolishness is wiser than men's wisdom, and what seems to be God's weakness is stronger than men's strength. (*1 Corinthians 1:23–5*).

There was normally three years of instruction before baptism. During this time Alexander would be attending the meetings of the church.

No Compromise

At the centre of the teaching lay the life and achievement of Jesus as he worked to reconcile the world to God again. That work had come to its climax in the cross and resurrection. But it was not easy to explain this to a person who had been brought up with pagan ideas of sacrifice. Jesus had not died to placate an angry God. He had gone to his death to show that no force in the entire universe was strong enough to break the love which united him with his Father. As man, he had died rather than compromise in any way with the sin which separated men from God. As God, he had shown that the divine love is stronger than death. As he rose from the dead, he had shown what human nature becomes when it is transformed by the living power of God's love.

During the course of his instruction, Alexander would find that his teachers were using ideas and words taken from ordinary everyday life. But they were stretching them and extending them to help him to understand God. 'Redemption' was a common idea in the ancient world; it meant the freedom given to a slave when his master released him, or release from the army for a soldier who had 'bought himself out'. 'Justification', was the verdict given in a court of law, when the accused was declared 'not guilty'. Through Jesus, people could be free again; they could be released from the terrible grip of sin, and be free to serve and love God. They could share in the pure innocence of God's own Son, and be forgiven all their sins, no matter how guilty they had been.

Union with the Son of God

Very early in the Church's history, before any of the Gospels had been written, Christians began to sum up their beliefs about Jesus Christ. They expressed their beliefs in ways which could be taught to converts and easily remembered. Later, these summaries of the Christian faith became creeds in which the truths about God were handed on down the generations. One of these very early summaries of the faith is quoted by Paul at the beginning of his Letter to the Colossians (see 1 : 15–20). It would certainly have been taught to new Christians by the teacher of the church in Colossae.

Again and again, in the writings of the early Christians, the phrase 'in Christ' occurs. If you read the letters of the New Testament, it quickly becomes clear that these people felt a very close relationship with Jesus. He was not just a supreme teacher. He was far more than the supreme model for a holy life. They felt that they were united to him. Each Christian believed that Jesus had united himself to each one of them. They were sharing in his life by an unbreakable union. (See p. 111.)

When they wrote to each other about this union, or talked about it, they used familiar comparisons. They compared it with a body and its many limbs and organs; a vine with its branches and fruit; a sacred temple built with many separate bricks. It was a union closer than the intimacy of husband and wife, and even more secure than the blood bond between parents and children. They were rough, earthenware vessels, but they were filled with the most precious of all contents—the powerful love and saving life of the Son of God himself and the Holy Spirit. Their union with Jesus took them into the life of the Holy Trinity, into the very heart of God.

The Fullness of God

They believed that this was what happened to them at baptism. In this simple rite, which could be performed wherever there was water available, their union with Jesus began, and nothing on earth could break it again. Yet it was only a beginning. For the union to grow and become effective, the Christian must respond to God's love with love of his own, no matter how feeble it might be. Then God would magnify that love until it reached into every remote corner of the Christian's life and personality, until he was filled with all the fullness of God.

Baptism was the climax of the convert's long period of instruction. As the time drew near, Alexander would be examined closely, to make sure that he appreciated the deep significance of the new life he was being offered. Then, as Easter approached, the candidates for baptism prepared for it with fasting and prayer. Except in emergency, when any Christian could perform the simple ceremony, baptisms were given only at Easter and, perhaps, Pentecost.

As the particularly solemn Easter meeting of the Christian Church moved towards its climax in the early hours of the morning of Easter Day, Alexander and the other converts gathered at the edge of the font, which was sunk in the floor with steps leading down into it. Stripping off their clothes, they went one by one down into the water. There, a presbyter laid his hand on Alexander's head while he made his profession of faith. This could have been as simple as the Ethiopian's reply to Philip in Acts 8:37: 'I believe that Jesus Christ is the Son of God.' Or it could be a full and long statement about the Holy Trinity, such as Peter gave towards the end of his sermon on the first day of Pentecost:

'God has raised this very Jesus from the dead, and we are all witnesses to this fact. He has been raised to the right side of God and received from him the Holy Spirit, as his Father had promised; and what you now see and hear is his gift that he has poured out on us. For David himself did not go up into heaven; rather he said:

> The Lord said to my Lord:
> Sit here at my right side,
> Until I put your enemies
> As a footstool under your feet.

All the people of Israel, then, are to know for sure that it is this Jesus, whom you nailed to the cross, that God has made Lord and Messiah!'

When the people heard this, they were deeply troubled, and said to Peter and the other apostles, 'What shall we do, brothers?' Peter said to them: 'Turn away from your sins, each one of you, and be baptized in the name of Jesus Christ, so that your sins will be forgiven; and you will receive God's gift, the Holy Spirit. For God's promise was made to you and your children, and to all who are far away—all whom the Lord our God calls to himself.' (*Acts 2:32–9*)

Then Alexander was immersed beneath the surface of the water in the font, while the presbyter said, 'I baptize you in the name of the Father and of the Son and of the Holy Spirit'. (See Matthew 28:19.) Standing again, the newly baptized Alexander mounted the steps from the font, put on a white garment, and was then anointed with consecrated oil by the presiding bishop.

The Eucharist

The ceremony was complete. God himself had made Alexander sure, by these outward signs, of his life in Christ. God had set him apart, and placed his mark of ownership upon him, and given him the Holy Spirit in his heart as the guarantee of all that he had in store for him (see 2 Corinthians 1:21–2). As a new Christian, Alexander could go forward into the most solemn part of the long night's events: the celebration of the Easter Eucharist at which he would make his first communion.

Perhaps we can best sum it all up with the words which Paul wrote to the Christians of Colossae, as he reminded them of their own baptisms:

> Since you have accepted Christ Jesus as Lord, live in union with him. Keep your roots deep in him, build your lives on him, and become ever stronger in your faith, as you were taught. And be filled with thanksgiving. See to it, then, that no one makes a captive of you with the worthless deceit of human wisdom, which comes from the teachings handed down by men, and from the ruling spirits of the universe, and not from Christ. For the full content of divine nature lives in Christ, in his humanity, and you have been given full life in union with him . . . For when you were baptized, you were buried with Christ, and in baptism you were also raised with Christ through your faith in the active power of God, who raised him from death.
> (*Colossians 2: 6–12*)

Whatever the differences which graded and separated people in the secular world, whether it was wealth, family, race or intelligence, Christians knew that their union with the risen Christ made them all one. And the same was true within the Church. There were many degrees of authority, responsibility and ability within the Christian community, from apostles and bishops right through to the most recently baptized members. Yet they knew that at the only level which really mattered they were all equal. Christ had given himself fully to each one of them, to share the power of the Holy Spirit of love with them, and bring each one to fulfilment in God.

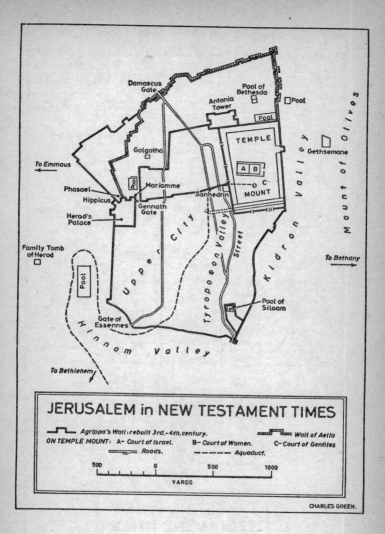

JERUSALEM in NEW TESTAMENT TIMES

Agrippa's Wall: rebuilt 3rd.–4th. century.   Wall of Aelia
ON TEMPLE MOUNT: A- Court of Israel.   B- Court of Women.   C- Court of Gentiles
Roads.   Aquaduct.

500   0   500   1000

YARDS

CHARLES GREEN.

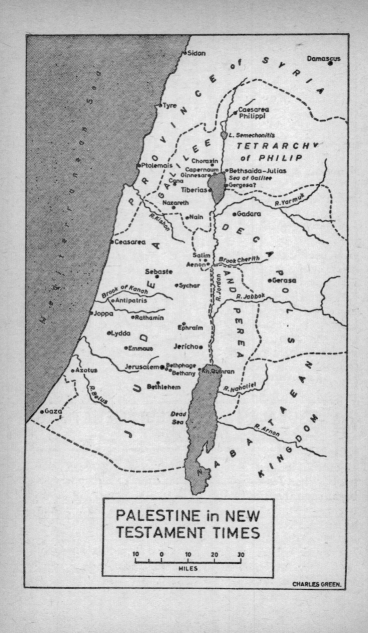

PALESTINE in NEW TESTAMENT TIMES

10   0   10   20   30
MILES

CHARLES GREEN.

Chapter 9

ABOUT PALESTINE

The most surprising thing about Palestine, when you visit it for the first time, is its smallness. No other area of the earth's surface has played such an important part in world history. In one way or another, the events which took place there have had an effect on everyone who is now living on this planet. Palestine is a sacred country for three of the world's most influential religions: Judaism, Christianity and Mohammedanism. Almost the entire action of the Bible takes place in it. Yet it is no more than 150 miles in length, from Dan to Beersheba, and 50 miles across at its widest point.

As you fly into Lod airport on a clear day, you can see right across the country, from the Mediterranean coast to the mountains on the other side of the Dead Sea; and you can almost see from top to bottom, from the headwaters of the River Jordan, above the Sea of Galilee, to the southern desert which separates Judea from Egypt. It is no more than a morning's comfortable drive in a modern car; an ancient army, marching up the great coast road from Egypt, could pass right through the country in a week.

Surprising Contrasts

Yet for all its smallness, it is a country of surprising contrasts. When Jesus made his last journey to Jerusalem, he began near the 9,000 ft Mount Hermon, capped by snow, twenty-five miles north of the Sea of Galilee. By the time he had passed down the Jordan Valley he had descended to the lowest point on the earth's surface, 1,300 feet below sea level. The valley is cut like a great, tilted trench, right down the eastern border of Palestine, until it ends in the salt-saturated waters of the Dead Sea.

The groves of dates, olives and oranges growing round Jericho, near the northern end of the Dead Sea, are a testimony to skilled irrigation and tenacious farmers, just as they were when Jesus passed as he climbed up the road from Jericho to Jerusalem. This notoriously dangerous road, winding through barren country, climbs nearly 4,000 feet between the two cities.

From Sea to Desert
From the Mount of Olives, Jerusalem is seen four-square, half a mile away across the Kidron Valley. When Jesus saw it, it was dominated by the Temple as it stood in all its magnificence on a great stone platform at the eastern edge of the city. Jerusalem had been a small, narrow town in David's time, as it clung to the Ophel ridge. But its walls had been enlarged five times in a thousand years until they enclosed an area three-quarters of a mile long and half a mile wide.

The ridge of mountains on which Jerusalem stands are the backbone of Palestine. They form the western wall of the Jordan trench on the one side, and on the other the ground falls away gently to the lush country along the coast of the Mediterranean. South from Jerusalem, through Bethlehem and Hebron, the mountain ridge peters out in rocky desert. North, through Samaria, the ridge dips into the fertile valley of Esdraelon, where Solomon's fortress of Megiddo stands guard, and then the ridge climbs up through Nazareth into the hills surrounding the Sea of Galilee.

Megiddo guards the pass where the great coast road crosses the shoulder of Mount Carmel as it juts out into the sea. That road is one of the oldest routes in the world. Journey southwards along it and you pass through the Philistine country (Palestine gets its name from the Philistines) until you reach Egypt. Northwards, one branch hugs the coast through Phoenicia and into Asia Minor. Phoenician traders sailing from Tyre and Sidon planted colonies all round the Mediterranean Sea in ancient times, and sailed as far as Britain for Cornish tin. Another branch of the road strikes inland past the Sea of Galilee to Damascus, and on into the great river plains of Mesopotamia where the Tigris and Euphrates drain into the Persian Gulf.

An Iron Grip

That road was the key to Palestine before aircraft transformed travel. Beyond the Jordan trench to the east, a great desert stretches to Mesopotamia. Even today parts of it are not even mapped. Palestine was the narrow corridor linking the mighty powers which ruled in Egypt and Mesopotamia, and each looked on Palestine as its first line of defence against the other. In their turn, Egyptians, Assyrians, Babylonians, Persians, Greeks and Romans all garrisoned Palestine and held the people in an iron grip. It was the key to the Middle East. In New Testament times Rome controlled it from Caesarea, the port on the Mediterranean coast where the legions were stationed. Local affairs were under the rule of the Herod family and the religious council which met in Jerusalem.

Palestine was a country of fortresses and small villages, and even the villages tried to be fortresses. The flat-topped houses huddled together within the surrounding wall, each house little more than a single room with an outside staircase leading up to the roof. The well, within the protection of the walls, and the single gate through which all the life of the village passed, were the centres of village life.

On the whole, there was very little industry. In a country which had to rely on what it could grow, most people were farmers, served by the village carpenter, the blacksmith and the potter. But there were no isolated farms. The fields were worked by people who could return to the safety of the village wall at night, when the gate was barred and a watch mounted.

Food and Crops
Barley and wheat were the main crops, together with
olives, dates and grapes. The first harvest of the year
came in the spring when the barley was reaped after the
cool, wet season. Almost all the rain fell during the
winter, when the moist winds blew in from the Mediterranean and Jerusalem was as wet as London. But the
summer was dominated by the harsh heat of the burn-
ing winds from the eastern desert beyond the Dead Sea.
Then the wheat ripened swiftly, to be harvested seven
weeks after the barley, and the fruit trees and grape vines
depended on the irrigation skills of their owners.

Bread was the staple food of most people, and meat
and fish occasional luxuries. The boy with a packed
lunch of five barley loaves and two small fishes, who was
in the crowd listening to Jesus, came from the district
near the Sea of Galilee with its small fishing industry.

Next to barley and wheat, olives were the most important crop. The oil pressed from the small, hard fruit
was used in a surprising number of ways. It provided fat
for cooking, and fuel for the small wick lamps which
hung in the houses. It was mixed with the flour or spread
on the bread, and it was the main cosmetic and medicine
for the poorer people who formed the majority of the
population. It is small wonder that anointing with olive
oil came to have such deep religious significance for the
Hebrews. The oil represented health and prosperity, and
a good olive crop meant comfort and security, for the oil
was easily stored and carried, and could be bartered
profitably. Kings and priests were solemnly anointed
with consecrated oil as a sign of their authority and
power, and the word for 'anointed one' became the most
sacred title known to the Hebrews—'Messiah'.

It was an uncertain world, with great differences in
wealth and power. The slaughter of the children of
Bethlehem by Herod's soldiers is all too real a picture
of the situation. And in a country where foreign occu-

pation forces and domestic rulers were exacting taxes, it was not surprising that rebellion and violence were so prevalent. Yet a religion of love and self-sacrifice sprang from this soil, to release people from their fears and give them real peace in the midst of their troubles.

Chapter 10

KEY WORDS AND IDEAS

The New Testament was written for people whose ordinary lives were often different from our own. Consequently, words and ideas, which had clear meanings for people living in Palestine or Greece two thousand years ago, may not be so clear to a modern reader of the New Testament. Some of these are listed below, with their meanings.

Abyss The place where all the living go at death, according to ancient Hebrew beliefs. Most Jews did not believe in resurrection of the dead, but only in this vague and shadowy existence after death. Later, some thought of it as a prison, where the dead were held captive by evil forces, or as the place where evil spirits were imprisoned while they awaited their final punishment.

Adultery Strictly speaking, Hebrew law defined adultery only as sexual intercourse with another man's wife, or with a woman to whom another man was betrothed. The punishment, for both of the people involved, was death by stoning.

Amen Literally, 'it is true'. Used of Jesus, it emphasizes that the promises made by God will be fulfilled in Jesus. Used by ordinary people, it is a sign of their acceptance of a truth, or of their desire to share in a prayer.

Angels There are many references to angels in the New Testament. They are presented as messengers of God, guardians of people on earth, and attendants of God in heaven. At a time when most people believed that the universe was full of personal and powerful forces of good and evil, belief in angels was unquestioned. The early Christian teachers had to emphasize that angels were creatures of God, not rivals equal to him in power. The danger of this kind of mistaken belief is as real now as it was then, so that it might be thought that angels have the power to save or damn people, or to intervene between God and mankind. Many of the mistakes about angels arise from attempts to picture them, rather than the belief in angels as such.

Annunciation The event described early in Luke's Gospel, when Mary was told that she was to be the mother of the Messiah. Mary's unconditional acceptance was the essential human response to God's action. It was the climax of the long history of imperfect human response as it is told in the Old Testament.

Apostle Literally, 'someone who is sent forth'. Jesus is called an apostle of God in the Letter to the Hebrews (3:1). This same idea lies behind the authority given to the apostles by Jesus, in his first appearance to them after his resurrection: 'Then Jesus said to them again, "Peace be with you. As the Father sent me, so I send you" ' (John 20:21). In a long explanation of the work of an apostle, Paul wrote, 'Here we are, then, speaking for Christ, as though God himself were appealing to you through us' (2 Corinthians 5:20). As the men who had known Jesus, and had been given authority by him, the apostles became the founders and leaders of the first groups of Christians. Strictly speaking, an apostle was 'a witness to the resurrection of the Lord Jesus. He must be one of those who were in our group during the whole time that the Lord Jesus travelled about with us, beginning from the time John preached his baptism until the day Jesus was taken up from us into heaven' (Acts 1:21–2). Paul was an apostle, even though he had not known Jesus during his time on earth, but at his conversion he did receive his authority as an apostle from the risen Jesus.

Ascension The end of Jesus' *visible* time on earth. The description of the ascension of Jesus, at the end of Luke's Gospel and at the beginning of the Acts of the Apostles, is told in terms of what people of the time believed about the world. They thought that the world was situated below heaven and above hell. The ascension of Jesus is to show his exaltation at the completion of his mission on earth.

Atonement This is a simple combination of the English words 'at-one' with 'ment' added to form a noun. It refers to the restoration of perfect relationships between God and his creation.

Baptism The ceremony of admission and cleansing when the candidate is immersed in water, or has water poured over his or her head. John the Baptist performed the rite as a symbol of penitence, but he did not claim any other power to forgive. The baptism given by Jesus and the Christian Church in the New Testament is a baptism of the Holy Spirit, and it has the power to transform the life of the person who is baptized. The New Testament letters show that the first Christians believed that baptism was the beginning of a union with the risen Jesus.

Bishop Literally, 'overseer' (*episkopos*), applied to the early Christian leaders in their responsibilities for the first Christian communities.

Blood In Hebrew thought, because blood carried the life of an animal, it was a symbol of life rather than of death. The blood of a sacrificed animal contained all the power of its sanctified life, and, when sprinkled over the worshippers, it brought them into contact with the power of God.

Centurion A non-commissioned officer of the Roman army, originally in charge of a hundred men.

Christ Literally, 'the anointed one'. The Greek translation of the Hebrew word 'Messiah'.

Church The Greek word translated by 'church' meant a formal assembly of the citizens of a town. In the New Testament, it means either all Christians, who are united together by their personal faith in Christ and their union with him; or it means the members of a local Christian community, such as 'the Church of God which is in Corinth' (1 Corinthians 1:2). The local communities were linked together by the leadership and rule of the apostles, by their common faith, based on the apostles' preaching, and by their common pattern of worship centred on the Eucharist.

Circumcision The practice of cutting off the foreskin of male children, which Jews performed to show that the child was a member of the people of the Covenant and shared in the promise made by God to Abraham. Originally it was probably an initiation rite to show that a boy had reached puberty and was ready for marriage. In the New Testament, circumcision is replaced by baptism, by which entry is gained into the community of the new covenant and a share in the promises of God fulfilled in Jesus. Unlike circumcision, baptism was never effective without the active faith of the person who had been baptized. (See p. 52.)

Confirmation Immediately after being baptized, the convert was anointed with consecrated oil by the bishop. This signified that he had been marked with God's seal of the Holy Spirit, and empowered to take up his responsibilities in the Christian community. With the growth of infant baptism, this part of the Christian ceremony of initiation was postponed until the person was old enough to understand his Christian responsibilities and accept them.

Conscience In the New Testament, this is the act by which a person decides what is right or wrong, and applies this knowledge to the particular circumstances of his situation. For conscience to be effective, a person must be clear about the moral principles of good and evil, and must also be able to apply them. Whenever he told parables, Jesus was persuading people to use their consciences to make a moral judgement and then apply it to their own lives.

Covenant Originally an agreement between people, the Hebrews used this idea to express the relationship between God and the people whom he had chosen. 'Covenant' is the same word as 'testament' when it is used in

'Old Testament' and 'New Testament'. The prophets, such as Jeremiah, came to see that the old covenant would have to be replaced, because the people had made it ineffective by their disobedience. If God was to work in his world through a covenant, it would have to be one which transformed people so that they were able to return his love. This was the new covenant which Jesus makes with all those who put their trust in him, sharing with them the perfect relationship which he has with his Father.

Cross The wooden execution gallows to which the Romans nailed or tied criminals and left them to die. The cross became the symbol of the power of God's love, which Jesus showed when he went willingly to such a terrible death rather than compromise with the people who would not accept him as Son of God.

Day The end of the world, when the Son of God will come again in glory to judge the world and complete the work of salvation.

Deacon Literally, 'one who waits at table'. In the early Church, deacons were officials appointed to help the apostles with the administrative work, such as distributing money to the poor. As is shown by the example of Stephen, they soon helped the apostles with their pastoral and priestly work as well, and became an important part of church organization. They were authorized for their work by the laying-on of hands.

Demon, devil The personification of evil. In the New Testament, particularly the Gospels, demons and devils are frequently mentioned when people are in the grip of forces opposed to God's will. Such language is understandable in an age which knew very little about psychology and the strength of the forces at work in a disordered human personality. As with angels, the main dangers of misunderstanding arise when attempts are made to picture such demons, and when it is believed that they are independent of God and equal to him in strength. If there is a personal power of good, as there is in God, there is every reason to accept the possibility of personal powers which attempt to oppose him. But a Christian, believing that there is only one God, who is supreme and the only creator, must therefore hold that such demons or devils are God's creatures, even if they are disobedient ones.

Disciple Someone who puts himself in the hands of a teacher. Most Jews would think that Jesus was just another wandering rabbi, or teacher, travelling about with his pupils. The twelve apostles were chosen from the much larger group of disciples.

Divorce Hebrew law contained no details about actions which might be reasons for divorce. It required only that a man who wished to divorce his wife should state it in writing. The only situation where a man could *not* divorce his wife was when he had wrongly accused her of adultery. A divorced woman was free to marry again, but could not return later to a previous husband. Divorce was easy to obtain in the pagan world, and in some countries it was also possible for the woman to divorce her husband. It can be seen that Jesus' teaching against divorce was in the sharpest contrast to the prevailing law and custom. The difficult passage in Matthew (19:9) probably refers to the Jewish law forbidding divorce of a wife falsely accused of adultery. Matthew was writing for Jewish readers, whereas the other Gospels were written for Gentiles who would not be concerned with such subtleties in Jewish law, so there would be no point in mentioning it.

Elder The Greek word is *presbyteros*, hence the English word 'presbyter'. Originally they were heads of families, but they appear in the early Christian communities as trusted men who share the responsibilities for administration with the apostles, especially in Jerusalem. Later, they appear to have been bishops of local churches, appointed by what we would now call the archbishop of a province.

Emmanuel The name of the child mentioned as a sign in

Isaiah 7:14. It means 'God is with us'. As Isaiah used it, the sign was a prophecy of disaster because the people had ignored God's presence and his power. The Hebrews and the first Christians saw this passage as a prophecy of the Messiah, who would save the faithful and rule as king when the disaster was over.

Faith Faith is the response of man to the love of God. It comes from a realization of human helplessness and of the power of God to save. In several places, the New Testament presents Abraham as the model of Christian faith, because he had complete confidence in God's promises. The resurrection of Jesus is the supreme reassurance of God's power and love. All the promises of God are fulfilled in Jesus, when he shares the fullness of his risen life with those who put their trust in him. This trust is faith.

Feasts and festivals The main Hebrew festivals were:

(1) *Passover and Unleavened Bread* (strictly speaking, these are two feasts joined together), which began on the fourteenth day of the spring month, the first month of the Hebrew year. Passover commemorated the escape from Egypt; Unleavened Bread was the first of the three harvest festivals, held at the beginning of the barley harvest.

(2) *Weeks*, or *Pentecost*, held fifty days after Unleavened Bread, at the beginning of the wheat harvest; it gets its name from the seven-week gap, and *pentecostos* is Greek for 'fiftieth'.

(3) *Tabernacles*, or *Tents*, when the fruit and olive crops were harvested, and the first wine of that year was ready to drink; it is named after the custom of sleeping out in the fields during this harvest, which then became a symbol of the journey through the wilderness after the escape from Egypt, when the people had to sleep in tents

(4) *New Year*, when the shofar, or ram's-horn trumpet was sounded.

(5) *Day of Atonement*, when the high priest made his annual entry into the Holy of Holies in the Temple, and a

bull was sacrificed as a sin offering by the high priest for his own and the other priests' sins. Then a goat was sacrificed for the people's sins, and another goat (the 'scapegoat') was driven out into the wilderness, carrying the people's sins with it. In each of the sacrifices, the blood of the victim was used as a cleansing agent, because it contained the sanctified life of the sacrificed animal. The Letter to the Hebrews draws on the ritual of the Day of Atonement to help explain the power of Jesus to save people from their sins.

(6) *The Sabbath*, the seventh and last day of each week (our 'Saturday'), when all work and travel was forbidden; it commemorated the work of creation, when God rested on the Sabbath, and the escape from Egypt when God rescued the Hebrews from forced labour.

The early Christians continued to keep the Jewish feasts and festivals at first, but *Sunday*, the day of the resurrection of Jesus, quickly replaced the Sabbath. *Easter* fell at the same time as Passover and Unleavened Bread, because Jesus was crucified at the Passover and rose from the dead two days later ('three days' by the Hebrew method of counting, which included the first and last day in its reckoning). In the early years, all baptisms, except in emergency, took place at Easter. *Pentecost* became the feast of the Holy Spirit because the first outpouring of the Holy Spirit took place at the feast of Pentecost (see Acts 2). It would seem that all other Christian feasts and festivals, including *Christmas*, belong to times later than the New Testament period.

Gehenna The Hebrew hell. It takes its name from the 'Valley of the Son of Hinnom' round the southern walls of Jerusalem. This was an ordinary valley which had terrible associations attached to it when the shrine of Moloch was built there more than seven centuries before the birth of Jesus. The worship of Moloch centred on human sacrifice of children by fire, even though this was strongly condemned by Hebrew law and by the prophets.

Gentile Anyone who was not of Jewish birth.

Gospel Literally, 'good news'. In the New Testament, the word is used primarily about the life and work of Jesus, both in heaven and on earth. The four Gospels are not biographies of Jesus, but selections of his teaching and actions, carefully arranged to illustrate the apostles' preaching of the 'good news' of salvation.

Grace From the Latin *gratus*, which means 'pleasing'. But the New Testament meaning is best seen from the Greek verb *charizesthai*, which means 'to grant something freely, as a favour'. God's love is given to mankind, solely because God gives it freely, not because it is deserved in any way. It was a deep misunderstanding about this which led to all the problems about Law amongst Jews and the first Christians. Even the most meticulous observation of laws and rules cannot establish a 'claim' or 'right' to God's saving power and love. (See p. 111.)

High Priest The head of the Hebrew priesthood at the Temple in Jerusalem, the only place where Hebrews permitted sacrifices to be offered. It was an annual appointment, made by the head of the civil government, but past holders of the office retained the title as a courtesy.

Hour Not a fixed unit of time, in the modern sense, but much more the appropriate or proper time for an event to happen. The Romans divided the daylight period into twelve equal periods, the nearest equivalent to an hour as we use it.

Hosanna From the Hebrew, 'we ask to be saved'. It was a word shouted by the crowds at the great feasts, especially Pentecost.

Jesus An ordinary Hebrew name, meaning 'God (Yahweh) is salvation'. In another form, 'Joshua' is the same name.

Judgement The main teaching about judgement in the New Testament is that people judge themselves, in effect, by the way in which they accept or reject Jesus as their saviour. John 1:10–13 sums this up very clearly. Jesus warned people strongly that they would be judged by the way in which they judged others, and in the Lord's Prayer he showed that people can only expect forgiveness from God if they first forgive other people for the injuries that they have suffered from them.

Kingdom of God King David brought in the brief period when the Hebrew people reached their highest point of national glory. Ever afterwards, they looked back with longing to that time when their people were united and free. This period became their model for the rule and age of the Messiah. In his teaching, Jesus started from these longings and from this model, and refined it so that his listeners could begin to understand the salvation which he was offering to them.

Law Basically, the system of rules and regulations authorized to govern people's lives. But it has a wider meaning in the Bible, where it also means the whole pattern of God's relationship with his creation, and the mighty actions by which he shows his power and love. This revelation of the character of God shows people the kind of lives which he expects of those who worship him.

Lord In its secular use, this carries the idea of authority and the power to release slaves. There is an important indication about the meaning which the first Christians gave to it when they used it of Jesus, for 'Lord' was the word used for Yahweh, the Hebrew name of God, in the Greek translation of the Old Testament.

Marriage By modern standards the ancient attitude to marriage, both amongst Hebrews and pagans, was very lax, because it was so easy to obtain divorce. The teaching of Jesus, that marriage is a union which cannot be broken, was a startling innovation. This unbreakable union was used by the early Christians as a model for the union between Jesus and his Church, which nothing could break. (See Ephesians 5:22–33.)

Messiah Literally, 'the anointed one', *christos* in Greek, from which comes the title 'Christ'. The Hebrews used consecrated oil to confer authority on kings and priests, as a sign of the power given to them by God to carry out their duties. The Messiah would be the supreme king and priest, authorized by God to bring in the final age of justice and salvation.

Miracle A miracle is a work which is thought to be beyond human ability. The early Christians recognized that Jesus played a key part in the creation of the world (see John 1:3 and Colossians 1:15–20), and that he had power over all created things and over nature itself during his life on earth. The miracles in the Gospels are selected and arranged to show that in his crucifixion and resurrection Jesus exhibited the same creative power to bring the world back to God again.

Money Several currencies were in circulation in Palestine and the Near East during New Testament times, but it must be remembered that most people managed well by bartering with each other, so that money as we know it played only a small part in their lives. Roman taxes had to be paid in Roman coinage, however, and the basic unit here was the denarius; this was a day's wage for a labourer. The Temple taxes in Jerusalem had to be paid in the special Temple coins, hence the need for money-changers in the outer courts of the Temple. Weights of metal, especially silver and gold, were the basis of coinage, and any coinage which had a good reputation for reliable weight and purity would be accepted readily.

Name Unlike our own customs, where a person's name is little more than an identity tab, the ancient world placed great significance on names. They expressed the character and authority of a person, and might be changed if there was an important change in a person's life. (See Mark 3:16–17, where Jesus changed the names of three of the apostles.)

Parable A parable is a story which makes just one main point and asks the hearer to make a decision about it. The point and the decision are then transferred to the hearer's own life and situation. When Jesus told parables he often left it to the audience to draw their own conclusions, for they were obvious, but he sometimes made the application himself, as in the parable of the Good Samaritan (Luke 10:25–37).

Passover The protection rite of the ancient Hebrews, which they used to ward off evil when moving camp and during the spring lambing period. A lamb was sacrificed and eaten in haste, after its blood (which contained the life of the lamb, now filled with God's power) had been smeared on the tent posts. The Passover became the rite which commemorated God's protecting and saving power during the escape from Egypt. Jesus was crucified and rose from the dead at the time of the Passover, to show that God was protecting and saving his people in a new and final way. The Last Supper was a Passover meal, and became the basis of the Christian Eucharist.

Pentecost See 'Feasts and Festivals'.

Pharisees A religious party or organization of Hebrews who were extremely strict in their interpretation of the Law. They first became prominent about a hundred and fifty years before the birth of Jesus, during the struggle against the Greek rulers, who wanted to impose the Greek way of life on the Hebrews. Unlike most Hebrews, the Pharisees believed in the resurrection of the dead. Paul was a highly trained Pharisee before his conversion. They were laymen, and were often politically opposed to the Hebrew priests.

Priest The priesthood was hereditary in the ancient Hebrew religion. Priests were responsible for the proper performance of the Temple sacrifices, and were the official guardians of the Hebrew religious laws. Because of the strict Hebrew law that only members of the tribe of Levi could be priests, and because of the possibility of confusion with the Hebrew religion, the very first Christians did not use the term 'priest'. But after the Temple had been destroyed by the Romans in AD 70, these difficulties no longer applied. The term comes into use with the Letter to the Hebrews. The early Church applied it to the work of Jesus, who is the source of all priesthood, and to those who shared in his ministry. So in one sense all baptized Christians are priests, through their union with Jesus. But it is more properly applied to those who are authorized and set apart to preside at the Eucharist, where the share in the sacrifice of Jesus is expressed.

Prophet An inspired teacher who can see how God's plan for mankind is working out and who tries to show this plan to others. To think that prophecy implies primarily an ability to see into the future can be misleading; it is more the ability to recognize how God makes his presence known now.

Psalm A hymn. The Old Testament psalms were the hymn book of the ordinary Hebrew people, and their main way of taking part in the Temple services. Most adult Hebrews would have known the psalms by heart, and Jesus alludes to them frequently in his teaching and in his own prayers.

Repentance The change of heart which produces sorrow for sin and the desire to be free from its power. Repentance and conversion are closely linked in the Gospels. Like faith, repentance is associated with the realization that human beings are helpless without God, and can only do harm to themselves and to others if they try to live without him.

Resurrection In the New Testament this is personal survival after death; not merely survival of just one part or aspect of a person, such as 'mind' or 'soul', but survival of the whole personality. This is shown by the resurrection of Jesus, when the apostles recognized him, touched him and saw him eat. In his resurrection, Jesus showed the unbreakable love which unites him, as Son of God, to the Father, and he also showed the perfection of human nature. The New Testament Christian hope is to share in the full perfection of the risen Jesus. This sharing in the risen life of Jesus has already begun, according to the New Testament, and will be completed after death, for those who have faith in Jesus.

Sabbath See 'Feasts and festivals'.

Sacrifice There were many different forms of Hebrew

sacrifice, from the offering of the first part of the harvest, to the dedication of animals. But in all cases, the object was to improve the relationship between the worshippers and God, or to thank God for the many examples of his love and protection. At their sacrifices, the Hebrews thanked God for the gift of life, and expressed their fellowship with God by sharing a meal with him. More deeply, they believed that the blood of an animal contained its life and when this life was given to God he filled it with his own life and power. By being sprinkled with the holy life-blood of the sacrificed animal, the people believed that they shared in God's life and were cleansed of their sins. There was nothing automatic or magical about this, for the Hebrews held that no sacrifice could help a person who had sinned so seriously as to cut himself off from God.

Our modern ideas about sacrifice are often pagan, connected mainly with death and loss, and with placating an angry God. This is not the belief about sacrifice in the New Testament, and it can lead to serious misunderstanding if such views are applied to the sacrifice of Jesus.

Sadducees The priestly party amongst the Hebrews, composed of the main priestly families, centred on the current high priest and his predecessors. They wielded considerable political power, often in opposition to the Pharisees. They did not believe in the resurrection of the dead.

Samaritans The inhabitants of Samaria, the part of Palestine north of Jerusalem, between Judea and Galilee. The original Hebrew inhabitants of Samaria were deported by the Assyrians more than seven hundred years before the birth of Jesus, and were replaced by people from other parts of the Assyrian empire. These newcomers accepted the Hebrew religion to a certain extent, but they and their descendants were treated as foreigners by the Hebrews of Judah. There was mutual and intense dislike between Jews and Samaritans in New Testament times.

Satan See 'Demon, devil'.

Scribe Originally, the scribes were the men who could write, and who were responsible for making copies of the scriptures, particularly the laws. In time, they acquired a reputation for knowledge of the law, and people turned to them for advice in legal matters. They were not a separate party and most of them belonged to the Pharisee group. It was only natural that they were hostile towards Jesus, who interpreted the law or changed it without (as they thought) having any authority to do so.

Second Coming The last act of Jesus, when he comes again in glory to judge the world and complete the work of salvation. The first Christians believed that Jesus had brought in the Messianic Age, the first stage of the Kingdom of God. This would be brought to an end at a time which only God knew; the universe would be destroyed and the saints would enter into their final glory. In the early years, many Christians gave up their jobs because they thought that the end of the world was near, but this belief slipped into the background as emphasis was placed on the presence of Christ in his body, the Church.

Son of God A title which the New Testament often applies to Jesus, even though it was not one of the titles normally used by Jews about the Messiah. It expresses the unique relationship between Jesus and the Father, shown most clearly in the crucifixion and resurrection. The Gospels refer to this relationship at the most solemn moments in Jesus' life on earth: at his baptism (Mark 1:11); his transfiguration (Mark 9:7); his trial before the High Priest (Mark 14:61-2); and at the end of the crucifixion (Mark 15:39).

Son of Man One of the main Jewish titles for the Messiah, taken from the description of the final arrival of the Messiah in triumph (see Daniel 7:13-14). Jesus applied it to himself at his trial before the High Priest (Mark 14:62) and so made it clear that he claimed to be the Messiah. It occurs frequently in the New Testament, where it combines the humanity of Jesus as he suffers to save the world, and the glory of Jesus as he shows the final authority, power and love of God.

Soul This is the personal self, which gives unity and character to a life. Perhaps the most important aspect of the idea of 'soul' is that of a pattern which runs through all the parts of a person's life, which makes an individual person distinct from everyone else. The Greeks thought that the soul would survive alone after death, and this way of thinking has the unfortunate result that only part of a person is thought to have any value. New Testament beliefs about the mystery of death centre on resurrection of the whole person, 'body and soul', rather than immortality of a mere part. Seen in this way, phrases such as 'saving your soul' imply the change needed in the whole of a person's way of life, if he or she is to be in full communion with God.

Spirit The basic meaning of the words translated by 'spirit', both in Hebrew and Greek, is 'breath' or 'wind'. In the first sense, it symbolizes the life of a person; in the second, it symbolizes power or force. It is thus the living source or power behind a person's actions. In the Christian life, as the New Testament sees it, the Holy Spirit guides people at this living centre of their personality, and cooperates with them. Thus their own feeble power to do what is right is magnified by the Holy Spirit so that they have the power to respond fully to God's love.

Synagogue From the Greek verb 'to gather together'. The synagogues were the meeting places for Jews, where they could worship, particularly on the Sabbath. They were also the places where Jewish children went to for school, under the direction of a local rabbi.

Temple The Temple in Jerusalem. The first Temple was built by Solomon to house the sacred Ark of the Covenant. A second Temple was built after the Babylonians destroyed the first one in 587 BC. In New Testament times the Temple was a new one, built on the same site by Herod. It was destroyed by the Romans in AD 70, and never rebuilt. It was the most sacred place on earth for Hebrews, and the only place where sacrifices could be offered. Consequently, the New Testament refers to Jesus as the new Temple of God.

Temptation An attraction towards evil. The ability to resist temptation is important evidence of the power of God's love. In the New Testament it is sometimes compared to the process of refining, in which gold or silver is heated to melting point to make sure that there is no impurity there.

Testament See 'Covenant'.

Tongue Usually speech or language, and so the intentions which are expressed through speech.

Word A title given to Jesus in the opening chapter of John's Gospel. It refers here to the effortless power shown by God at the creation of the world, when he only had to speak the word of command in order to create. Jesus possessed this power, and he linked the world to God. As he assisted in the original work of creation, so now he brings God's loving power into the world. He is the source of the new creation, by which the world is brought back to God again, to find its fulfilment in obedience to God's love.

World This is often used in the New Testament to mean a system or set of influence which opposes God or tries to ignore him. This is the sense in which Jesus uses it, for example, when he says, 'The world will make you suffer. But be brave! I have defeated the world!' (John 16:33.) In another sense, 'the world' is all mankind, the supreme object of God's love. It was for the sake of 'the world' that Jesus Christ became man, died and rose from the dead (see John 3:16–17).

Part II

INTRODUCTIONS TO THE
BOOKS OF THE NEW TESTAMENT

THE GOSPEL OF MATTHEW

Who Is Matthew?

It is unusual for people today to change their names. If they do so they are required to register the change legally by deed poll. It was not unusual for the people we meet in the Bible. Abram became Abraham. Simon's name was changed by Jesus to Peter. Saul after his conversion, was known as Paul.

In the Gospels of Mark and Luke we are first introduced to Matthew under the name given him by his parents. 'As [Jesus] walked along, he saw a tax collector, Levi, the son of Alphaeus, sitting in his office. Jesus said to him, "Follow me." Levi got up and followed him' (Mark 2:13–14). 'After this Jesus went out and saw a tax collector named Levi, sitting in his office. Jesus said to him, "Follow me." Levi got up, left everything and followed him' (Luke 5:27–8). Only in the Gospel of Matthew are we straight away given the name by which we know him. 'Jesus left that place, and as he walked along he saw a tax collector, named Matthew, sitting in his office. He said to him, "Follow me." And Matthew got up and followed him' (9:9). The name Matthew means 'Gift of God'.

Sitting in his Office

So Matthew was a civil servant, one of that hated group called by the Gospel writers 'publicans'. (This word bears no relationship with the work we associate today with 'publican'. It simply indicates that such a man was concerned with the collection of 'public' money.) Tax collectors were hated not only because they were collaborators and quislings, employed by the occupying Romans. They were hated because, in addition, they were often believed to be guilty of extortion. Matthew was, in fact, employed by King Herod, a puppet of the Romans. His office was situated in Galilee on the main road leading from the North (Syria) to the South (Egypt). He was concerned with extracting import and export duty on the goods that passed along this route. Was it humility on the part of Matthew that led him to omit from his Gospel the touching sequel that followed his call? His first action was to introduce Jesus to his 'club' —a group of equally despised publicans and sinners. Perhaps Matthew had no other friends. (You can read about this in Luke 5 : 27–32.)

Who Wrote Matthew's Gospel?

To ask who wrote Matthew's Gospel may seem at first sight to be a stupid and unnecessary question. But as we have seen elsewhere (pp. 22–6), the Gospels, as we have them today, were not written down within a short time of Jesus' death and resurrection. In the days when very few people could read and write the first accounts of our Lord's words and deeds were memorized. Only later were these accounts put into written form.

Scholars speak of our St Matthew's Gospel as the 'Greek Matthew' because many of them believe that it is an edited translation of an original Gospel of Matthew written in Aramaic, the spoken language of the Jews. Of course, there is much debate among scholars, but the most common belief is that the Gospel we have today may have grown out of an earlier Gospel, put together by the apostle Matthew.

'The Greatest Book Ever Written'

That is how this Gospel has been described. Most of the various phrases from the New Testament with which people are familiar come from this Gospel. It is the most comprehensive of the four. Perhaps Matthew's office work of balancing accounts gave him the sense of order and balance constantly apparent here. He puts together the words of Jesus given at different times and on different occasions into five great sermons:

The Sermon on the Mount—Chapters 5–7
A disciple's code of conduct—Chapter 10
The Parables—Chapter 13
Forgiveness of those who harm us—Chapter 18
The coming of the Kingdom—Chapters 24–25

He weaves around these collected sayings of Jesus the story of the coming of God's Kingdom (better translated as 'Kingship') in the person of Jesus.

The Jesus of Matthew is a 'teaching Jesus', the new Moses. Notice how Matthew situates the first great proclamation (Chapters 5–7) on a mountain top—just as Moses brought the Law of God from another mountain, Mount Sinai, and taught with the authority of God.

'You have heard that men were told in the past, "Do not murder . . ." But now I tell you: whoever is angry with his brother will be brought before the judge' (5:21). 'You have heard that it was said, "Do not commit adultery." But now I tell you: anyone who looks at a woman and wants to possess her is guilty of committing adultery with her in his heart' (5:27). 'You have heard it said . . . but I say to you . . .' occurs six times in this one sermon. Yet Jesus also says, 'I have not come to do away with them [the Law of Moses and the teaching of the prophets], but to give them real meaning' (5:17). (It is also interesting to note Matthew's inclusion of our Lord's words: 'Why should you expect God to reward you, if you love only the people who love you? Even the *tax collectors* do that!' (5:46—authors' italics)

For Convert Jews

Matthew is writing for convert Jews and the more we can assume the outlook of those people, the more will this Gospel speak to us. We must remember that a Jew in the early Christian era was steeped in the Old Testament. (See pp. 38ff.)

This is one reason why the Gospel of Matthew is so

full of references to the Old Testament, ('the Law and the prophets'). As you read Matthew you will frequently come across such phrases as, 'This was done to make come true what [the prophet Isaiah] [the scriptures] had said.' Matthew is pointing to Jesus as the fulfilment of the Old Testament. Jesus, he says, brings about the coming of a new Kingdom for the Jews. Many, however, refused to believe in him. But those who have accepted him in faith make up the new people, the new Israel.

Perhaps it is because Matthew is himself a Jew that he does not hesitate to castigate the leaders of his own race. We can read for example the withering words of Jesus against the hypocrisy of the Pharisees (Chapter 23). But as we read we should beware of the temptation to say, 'Thank God, I am not like these Pharisees.' Rather, we should allow our petty shams and hypocrisies also to be exposed to the gaze of Christ.

How to Read Matthew

Start with the Sermon on the Mount. One often hears people say, 'I wouldn't exactly call myself a fanatical Christian, but I do believe in the Sermon on the Mount.' Surely such people cannot have read Matthew 5–7. For these words of Jesus make such exacting demands on personal and social behaviour as could transform the world.

THE GOSPEL OF MARK

Who Was Mark?

John Mark is mentioned several times in the New Testament.* A Jew, born in Jerusalem, he first became the travelling companion of Paul until a difference of opinion separated them temporarily (see Acts 15:37). Later, he was such an ardent member of Peter's congregation in Rome that after Peter's death (about the year 65) he used Peter's accounts of Jesus' words and sayings as the principal source for his Gospel.

An early Christian, Papias, described Mark's Gospel in these words: 'Mark, indeed, who became the interpreter of Peter, wrote accurately, as far as he remembered them, the things said or done by the Lord, but not however in order. For he had neither heard the Lord nor been his personal follower, but at a later stage, as I said, he had followed Peter who used to adapt his teaching to the needs [of the time] but not as though he were drawing up a connected account.'

If we accept this tradition that Mark was Peter's interpreter, then we must conclude that in his sermons Peter concentrated more on what Jesus *did* than on what he *said*. For Mark's Gospel is packed with action and contains fewer of Jesus' discourses than appear in Matthew and Luke.

It is worth noting that Mark's Gospel was probably the first to be written. Even though in our New Testament it is placed after the Gospel of Matthew, it was almost certainly written before Matthew's and both he and Luke used Mark's Gospel as a guide when they later came to construct their Gospels.

* See for example, Acts 12:12, 25; 13:5; 15:37.

The Way He Wrote

Every writer has a style of his own. Mark's style is not polished. His way of writing is similar to the unsophisticated story-telling of children. He uses fairly short sentences with few subordinate clauses; his Gospel reads more like the spoken than the written word.

This confirms the traditions mentioned above, that Mark used Peter's sermons as his main source. Indeed, if some of the passages are transposed into 'we' instead of 'they', it is not altogether fanciful to believe that we catch the echo of Peter's voice. For example: 'The apostles [we] returned and met with Jesus and told him all [we] they had done and taught. There were so many people coming and going that [we] Jesus and his disciples didn't even have time to eat. So he said to [us] them, "Let us go off by ourselves to some place where we will be alone and you can rest awhile." So [we] they started out in a boat by [ourselves] themselves to a lonely place' (6:30–2).

Then, Then, Then

Mark does not concern himself overmuch with the actual succession of events in the order in which they occurred. He strings together a whole series of largely unrelated incidents, joining them to each other (rather as children do) by the use of the word 'then'.

His attention to detail colours these brief cameos of Jesus' work. It is worth comparing in Matthew and Mark accounts of the same event to see how Mark's insertion of just a touch of detail makes the action live. For example, read the account of the storm at sea in Matthew (8:23–7) and then in Mark (4:35–41).

Mark's Readers

It is generally thought that Mark's Gospel was written in Rome for Romans. It is not strange that it was originally in Greek, for the non-Jewish Christians of Rome more frequently used Greek as their first language. As you read the Gospel you will come across evidence that his readers were unfamiliar with Jewish customs (see, for example, Mark 7:3ff).

Mark was not attempting to bring his readers to a belief in Jesus Christ, for they were believers already. Perhaps, rather, his Gospel is aimed at strengthening their faith in him despite the ruthless persecution of Christians under the Roman emperor, Nero, thirty-four years after the crucifixion.

This presentation may be the reason why Mark devotes so much of his Gospel (one fifth) to an account of the passion and death of our Lord. He is saying, Jesus Christ, the mighty Son of God, allowed himself to be treated in this barbarous way. Are we to expect an easier death? Jesus himself said, 'If anyone wants to come with me, he must forget himself, carry his cross, and follow me. For the man who wants to save his own life will lose it; but the man who loses his life for me and for the gospel will save it' (8:34). These words would not be an empty spiritual cliché for people who expected at anytime to die violently and cruelly. (See also I Peter 2:21 and I Peter 3:12.)

How to Read Mark's Gospel

This is the shortest of the Gospels. It could be read in less time than it takes most people to assimilate the contents of a Sunday 'quality' paper; just less than an hour. To read it at one sitting would provide you with a remarkable experience. You would sense the urgency of the 'Good News about Jesus Christ, the Son of God' (1:1). And what is this Good News? That this simple Galilean who took it upon himself to help the blind, the lame, the deaf and dumb, is truly the Son of God (1:11; 9:7).

As you read the Gospel, you will sense the inescapable pressure of the crowds, the hurried comings and goings. You will notice how the admiration for Jesus in the first half of the Gospel (up to Chapter 8) turns to a hostility that brought about his death. But this death is not the end. 'The army officer, who was standing there in front of the cross, saw how Jesus had cried out and died. "This man was really the Son of God!" he said' (15:39).

THE GOSPEL OF LUKE

Who Is Luke?

'Do your best to come to me soon,' wrote Paul from prison. 'For Demas fell in love with this present world and has deserted me . . . Crescens went to Galatia, and Titus to Dalmatia. Only Luke is with me' (Timothy 4:9).

So Luke, the one non-Jewish contributor to the New Testament was the close companion of Paul and, like Mark (see p. 85), accompanied him on some of his journeys. These journeys are described by Luke in his second book, the Acts of the Apostles. This book is a continuation of his Gospel but, in our Bibles, the two parts are separated by the Gospel of St John.

Our Dear Doctor

Paul in another letter (to the Christians at Colossae) spoke of Luke as 'our dear doctor'. Certainly there are hints throughout his Gospel that this was in fact his profession. For example it is interesting to see the way Luke alters somewhat a comment of Mark (from whom he borrowed much material), in order to avoid a slur on the good name of doctors. Mark writes, 'There was a woman who had suffered terribly from severe bleeding for twelve years, even though she had been treated by many doctors. She had spent all her money, but instead of getting better she got worse all the time' (Mark 5:25). Luke more prudently writes: 'A certain woman was there who had suffered from severe bleeding for twelve years; she had spent all she had on doctors, but no one had been able to cure her' (8:43).

Luke, the doctor, is very much alive to human needs and, in his portrayal of Jesus, he emphasizes the fact that Jesus is the saviour of all men, that Jesus is humanity's doctor. 'The Son of Man came to seek and to save the lost' (19:10). ' "Why do you drink with tax collectors and outcasts?" they asked. Jesus answered them: "People who are well do not need a doctor, but only those who are sick. I have not come to call the respectable people to repent, but the outcasts" ' (5:31–32).

A Revolutionary

Most of Luke's contemporaries despised the poor. Riches were regarded as a reward from God for a virtuous life. If a person was poor, it was because he was out of favour with God.

Luke cuts right across this way of thinking and brings out the compassion of Jesus for the poor and the outcast. 'Happy are you poor: the Kingdom of God is yours! Happy are you who are hungry now: you will be filled!' (6:20–1). This echoes the revolutionary sentiments of Mary's hymn adapted by Luke:

He stretched out his mighty arm
And scattered the proud people with all their plans.
He brought down mighty kings from their thrones
And lifted up the lowly.
He filled the hungry with good things,
And sent the rich away with empty hands. (*1:51*)

The Faith of Women

Not only did most of Luke's contemporaries despise the poor, they also paid little regard to the personal dignity of women. Thanks to this Gospel, we have some touching snapshots of many of the women whose response to Jesus was one of deep faith: Elizabeth, Anna, Martha and her sister Mary, Mary Magdalene, the widow of Nain. Most important of all, Mary of Nazareth who 'remembered all these things, and thought deeply about them' (2:19). How impoverished our appreciation of

Mary's character would be if we did not have the narratives about the infancy of Jesus which are given such prominence in Luke.

How to Read this Gospel

What else have we to thank Luke for? The parables of the Good Samaritan, the Publican and the Pharisee, the Prodigal Son (and many other parables), the healing of the ten lepers, the story of Zacchaeus, the meeting on the road to Emmaus. These are just a few of the glimpses we are given of Jesus and his message.

To discover just how much in debt we are to this 'dear doctor', first read the account given in Matthew (27:44) of two thieves crucified alongside of Christ; then turn to Luke (23:39–43) and there see the wonderful last-minute offer of pardon.

Indeed, the best introduction to this Gospel might well be to read some of the paragraphs, proper to Luke alone, dealing with forgiveness:

The sinner in Simon's house	(7:36–50)
The Prodigal Son	(15:11–32)
Zacchaeus	(19:1–10)
'Forgive them, Father'	(23:34)
'In Paradise with me'	(23:39–43)

Other Things to Notice

Luke displays a great interest in Jerusalem. Half-way through his narrative he writes, 'As the days drew near when Jesus would be taken up to heaven, he made up his mind and set out on his way to Jerusalem' (9:51). From then on, Luke weaves his narrative around Jesus' last journey to his death in the holy city. In part two of his work, the Acts of the Apostles, Luke is going to lead his reader from Jerusalem to Rome.

Of equal prominence in the two works are the numerous references to the Holy Spirit. This is hardly surprising when we remember Luke's relationship with Paul who is continually drawing people's attention to the power of the Spirit in their lives.

A Domestic Gospel

One writer has described Luke's account of the Annunciation (1:26–38) as 'the most perfect short story ever written'. There are many such stories in this Gospel. Many of them have a touch of domesticity. From the lake of Gennesaret and the fields of Palestine, Luke takes us indoors and allows us to see Jesus dining among friends in the intimacy of their homes. Perhaps the most moving of those occasions is the supper Jesus shared with his disciples on the road to Emmaus. (24: 18–32)

In the opening sentence of his Gospel, Luke dedicates his work to 'Theophilus'. We know nothing about Theophilus, but if he were a Gentile convert who asked Luke to write this 'orderly account' so full of joy and serenity, then indeed his name deserves to live on.

THE GOSPEL OF JOHN—I

Who Is John?

Zebedee had two sons James and John, who helped him
to fish the lake of Galilee. These boys were given a nick-
name by Jesus: 'Sons of thunder', because when some
Samaritans refused to believe in Jesus they asked for
lightning to strike the village. James and John together
with Peter witnessed events in Jesus' life denied to the
other apostles. For example, they were with Jesus when
he was transfigured in glory, and in the garden of Geth-
semane it was these three whom Jesus invited to take
their place close to him in his mental agony. There were
other occasions too when, of the twelve apostles, they
alone were invited to accompany Jesus.

It was John who, at Jesus' trial in the courtyard of the
High Priest, arranged for Peter to be admitted (18:16).
If you turn to this Gospel reference you will see we are
presuming that (to quote this Gospel), the 'disciple whom
Jesus loved' is, in fact, John. While there are some who
argue against this traditional belief, it is difficult to understand why the apostle John is not mentioned by name
once in this Gospel, unless the writer is indeed John
himself.

To his Home

It was John who stood by the cross with Mary.

Standing close to Jesus' cross were his mother, his
mother's sister, Mary the wife of Clopas, and Mary
Magdalene. Jesus saw his mother and the *disciple he
loved* standing there; so he said to his mother,
'Woman, here is your son.' Then he said to the disciple, 'Here is your mother.' And from that time the

disciple took her to live in his home. *(19:25-7—
authors' italics)*

It was John who outran Peter to the tomb on Easter
morning. 'The two of them were running, but the other
disciple ran faster than Peter and reached the tomb
first' (20:4). It was John who from the boat recognized
Jesus when he prepared breakfast for them on the shore:
'The disciple whom Jesus loved said to Peter, "It is the
Lord"' (21:7).

What Happened to John?

After Jesus' resurrection we know that for a time he
worked with Peter (see Acts 3:1–10). He shared a prison
sentence with Peter. Of the rest of his life we know very
little. It has long been believed that his later years were
spent in Ephesus—a town on the Mediterranean coast of
present-day Turkey, not far from Rhodes. Many people
think that this is where his Gospel was born—some sixty
years after Jesus' death and resurrection.

An Old Bishop

To illustrate the way in which we believe John's Gospel
was formed, let us take an imaginary but quite possible
example. An elderly bishop retires from the active life
of the apostolate at the age of eighty. He has not long
celebrated the golden jubilee of his priesthood. In his
retirement he looks back over his life and he remem-
bers particularly the preparation for the priesthood given
him in the seminary. This training has been the foundation of nearly all his preaching. As he looks back he
sees much more clearly than he did at the time, the
meaning of his first introduction to the way of Christ.
He jots down some of his memoirs and his reactions to
the events of his early days in the priesthood.

Because these memoirs are enhanced by his experience they are richer by far than any diary he may have
made of the events at the time they happened. After his
death, his friends come across these writings and decide

to publish them. They also remember many of the
sermons and the anecdotes he used to illustrate them,
so they incorporate these also into the body of the book.

A Vivid Memory

Thus could it have been with John's Gospel. But how
can anyone remember things so accurately over such a
span of time, the reader may ask? The personality of
Jesus was not one to be forgotten, especially when the
one recalling the event was afterwards in daily communion with his Lord.

Moreover this same Lord had promised, 'The Holy
Spirit . . . will make you remember all that I have told
you' (14:26). It is well known that most old people,
while they may not remember what happened yester-
day, can recall without difficulty details from the distant
past. As you read the Gospel of John, you will come
across many vivid details of Jesus' life. 'Jesus rose from
the table, took off his outer garments, and tied a towel
round his waist' (13:4). 'Jesus said to [Judas], "Hurry
and do what you must!" ' . . . Judas accepted the bread
and went out at once. It was night' (13:27–30). 'It was
cold, so the servants and guards had built a charcoal fire
and were standing around it . . .' (18:18). '. . . the other
disciple ran faster than Peter' (20:4).

So That You May Believe

As we have seen, the four evangelists were not concerned
to write a biography of Jesus listing in chronological
order all he said and did. Each of them selected from
their material very carefully. This is most evident in
John. His Gospel is unlike the other three. Matthew,
Mark and Luke give a fairly direct account of some of
Jesus' deeds and words. They leave the reader to work
out the implications for himself. Locked away in John's
memory was a vast amount of material which he could
have used. 'Jesus did many other mighty works in his
disciples' presence which are not written down in this

book' (20:30). A disciple adds in the postscript to John's Gospel that if all the things Jesus did were written down 'I suppose that the whole world could not hold the books that would be written' (21:25). John decided to choose from all this material a comparatively small number of events, and not only describe the events but interpret them, to bring out their deeper significance. It is as though John is saying: I am writing down these things so that you may look beyond these events and there discover that Jesus is the answer to the questions of life. 'These have been written that you may believe that Jesus is the Messiah, the Son of God, and that through this faith, you may have life in his name' (20:31).

THE GOSPEL OF JOHN—II

Seven Signs

As we have seen in the previous chapter, John was concerned, for the greater part of his Gospel, to select a comparatively small number of incidents and interpret the significance of these events. These seven signs (as John calls them) are:

The miracle of Cana	(2:1–12)
The curing of the nobleman's son	(4:46–54)
The cure of the paralytic	(5:1–17)
The feeding of the five thousand	(6:1–14)
The walking on the water	(6:16–21)
The cure of the man born blind	(9:1–41)
The raising of Lazarus	(11:1–44)

His aim is twofold: to bring those who are not yet believers to accept Jesus as the Messiah, the Son of God; and to help Christians realize that they do not need to envy those who saw and met Jesus in bodily form. For Jesus lives on in the sacraments and worship of his Church.

Of course, we will look in vain in John's Gospel for the word 'sacrament' (or for that matter 'Church'), but references to the new life God gives through Jesus abound. Jesus' talk with Nicodemus (notice how he comes in from the dark—'it was night'—to see the Light of the world) is about the new life of baptism (Chapter 3). The incident of the man born blind who is helped to see after having washed at the pool of Siloam, again refers to the light the Christian enjoys at baptism (Chapter 9). Jesus' sermon on the bread of life is obviously directed towards the Eucharist.

To the Christians of Ephesus who may well have said to John, 'If only we had been there with you,' John recalls Jesus' words to Thomas, 'Do you believe because you see me? How happy are those who believe without seeing me!' (20:29)

Event Accompanied by Discourse

As you read this Gospel you will notice that very often the sign is accompanied or followed by a discourse. For example, Jesus feeds five thousand and immediately describes himself as the bread of life. After the man born blind has been cured, he is excommunicated by the 'blind' religious leaders of the synagogue. Jesus describes himself (Chapter 10) as the true leader, the good shepherd.

At the raising of Lazarus from the dead, Jesus describes himself as the 'resurrection and the life'.

The only event in Jesus' life which of its nature could not naturally be accompanied or followed by a discourse explaining its significance was his own death and resurrection. And so this discourse is situated by John at the Last Supper (Chapters 14–17) immediately *before* the sign.

I Am

The two short words 'I am' were full of significance for the Jews. They form the root of the word they used for 'God'. 'I am who I am' God had said to Moses (Exodus 3:14). One frequently finds 'I am' in John's Gospel:

'I am the bread of life' (6:35). 'I am the light of the world' (8:12). 'Before Abraham was born, I am' (8:58). 'I am the door for the sheep' (10:7). 'I am the good shepherd' (10:14). 'I am the resurrection and the life' (11:25). 'I am the way, I am the truth, I am the life' (14:6). 'I am the real vine' (15:1).

The Challenge

If you have read St Matthew's Gospel you will not have easily forgotten Jesus' words to the Pharisees (Chapter 23). In John's Gospel Jesus also condemns the blindness

of the Jewish leaders, but whereas in Matthew the Pharisees are apparently a silent audience, in John they argue
back. John calls those who deliberately blind themselves
to Jesus' claim, 'the Jews'. This is not a racial description but the title (like 'the world') which John reserves
for those who deliberately reject Christ.

This question, 'Do you accept me or not?' is a recur-
ring theme. It admits of no compromise answer. This
challenge of faith which Jesus presents in almost every
page of the Gospel, is not of historical interest only.
Today we too are challenged to make this decision for or
against Jesus.

How to Read John's Gospel

One point of entry into John's Gospel would be to begin
by reading two of the 'signs'. The cure of the man born
blind (Chapter 9) followed by Jesus' description in the
subsequent chapter of the good shepherd (a contrast to
the bad 'shepherds' of Chapter 9).

Then turn to the raising of Lazarus (Chapter 11). Do
not be content simply to read John's words as though
you were reading a newspaper report. He wants you to
read between the lines. Look out for the delicate hints
of inner meaning that John suggests in order to add
depth to his account. Sometimes he fears that we may
overlook these hints and cannot resist pointing them out
to us. For example, 'Don't you realize', said the High
Priest (after the raising of Lazarus) 'that it is better for
you to have one man die for the people, instead of the
whole nation being destroyed?'—and here John gives us
the clue by adding. '(Actually, he did not say this of his
own accord; rather, as he was High Priest that year, he
was prophesying that Jesus was about to die for the
Jewish people, and not only for them, but also to bring
together into one body all the scattered children of God)'
(11:50).

Since Lazarus' resurrection was the immediate cause
of the plot to kill Jesus, it is likely that you will want to

read on from there to the end. Once having started the account of the passion in John, it is impossible not to continue. Notice the increasing tension as he describes the way in which Pilate struggles between the demands his conscience makes to have Jesus acquitted and the demands of the mob to have Jesus condemned.

And then the sombre but unadorned account of the crucifixion. (When you read the word 'Woman'—not 'Mother'—in 19:26, you will surely be reminded of the 'woman' in 2:4, whose 'hour' has now arrived.)

In Chapter 20, spring has arrived. New life, joy, peace, friends, reconciliation.

The Sublime

After we have read a novel, very rarely do we want to read it a second time. The fascinating characteristic of the Gospels is that no matter how often we read them, we always want to read them again, and, for sure, we will discover something new.

While this is true of all the Gospels, perhaps in the Gospel of John it is most obviously verified.

One word has been used more frequently than any other to describe John's Gospel, and that word is 'sublime'.

THE ACTS OF THE APOSTLES

Dear Theophilus

This is how Luke begins the Acts of the Apostles: 'Dear Theophilus: In my first book I wrote about all the things that Jesus did and taught, from the time he began his work until the day he was taken up to heaven . . .' (1:1–2).

Now, in this second part, Luke wants to recount what then happened to the apostles (especially Peter and Paul) and to all those who believed in Jesus.

The first part of Luke's writing (the Gospel) told the story of Jesus, beginning with his preaching in Galilee and ending with his death and resurrection in Jerusalem. In Acts, Luke begins in Jerusalem and ends in Rome. He concludes his account abruptly as though he is saying: I could tell you more but now I can lay down my pen. I have traced the progress of belief in Jesus from its humble beginnings in unknown Nazareth to its proclamation in Rome, the centre of the world. There is nothing more I want to add.

The Holy Spirit

This final sentence of Acts describes Paul's preaching in Rome: 'He preached about the Kingdom of God and taught about the Lord Jesus Christ, speaking with all boldness and freedom' (28:31). Luke is writing of an event that took place in the year 62 or 63, a mere thirty years after the crucifixion.

We are not surprised in our day at the speed with which news travels. President Kennedy's death was known throughout the world within minutes of its happening. In the first Christian century, the communication of news and ideas was much slower.

That this 'son of a carpenter', hanged as a criminal in a remote province, should be confessed in sophisticated Rome as 'the Lord' in such a short time and at the risk of death cannot be the result of mere human endeavour. It must be the work of the Holy Spirit.

This chronicle of Luke's describes something of the way in which the Holy Spirit guided the early Church in her mission to bring the 'Good News of Jesus' to every creature. For this reason Acts has been described as 'the Gospel of the Holy Spirit'. As you read this exciting account you will constantly come across these 'interventions' of the Spirit.

Critical Problems

Jesus withdrew only his visible presence from the apostles on Ascension Day. He was not going to leave them. 'I will be with you always,' he had said, 'to the end of the age' (Matthew 28:20). He had not told them everything. He had given them no detailed plan of campaign. 'I have much more to tell you, but now it would be too much for you to bear. But when the Spirit of truth comes, he will lead you into all the truth' (John 16:12–13).

There were many problems facing the apostles, to which there were no ready-made answers. The most critical of these was whether Gentiles (that is, non-Jews) might be admitted into the Church. To us it may seem obvious that the Christian Church is for all men. To Peter and Paul and their contemporaries the question was by no means so simple. Jesus himself was a Jew and had he not said, 'Do not think I have come to do away with the Law of Moses and the teaching of the prophets. I have not come to do away with them, but to give them real meaning' (Matthew 5:17). The apostles and first disciples had been brought up in the Jewish belief that their religion was for Jews only. It is not surprising then that after Pentecost 'every day they continued to meet as a group in the Temple' (Acts 2:46). Only later did they realize that 'the Way' (the name they gave to those who believed in Jesus) was more than an adjunct to Judaism: it had to exist on its own.

You can read in Chapter 10 how the Holy Spirit helped Peter to reach this conclusion.

How to Read This Book

Acts is a well told story. One exciting event is succeeded immediately by another. The book is divided into six main sections:

	Chapters
The infant church in Jerusalem	1– 6
The first step away from Jerusalem	6–10
The church in Antioch—mainly about Paul's first journey, but a return visit to Jerusalem to see the First Council in action	10–15
Paul's second journey	15–18
Paul's third journey	18–21
Paul's arrest and his journey to Rome	21–28

The first half of Acts is thus concerned mainly with Peter; the second half, devoted almost entirely to Paul.

Luke was for much of the time Paul's travelling companion and the journeys which Luke shared with Paul are described in the first person plural. These are the famous 'we' passages. Since Acts, at least from Chapter 10 onwards, is a travelogue it will make much more sense if you are able to refer often to the map at the beginning of the book (pp. 4–5).

Where to Start

Luke's style is vivid. To catch something of his ability as a raconteur, first read the account he gives of Peter's escape from prison (Chapter 12). Notice how Peter, dazed from sleep, needs to be told to tighten his belt, tie his sandals, put on his cloak. Notice too Rhoda's very feminine reaction as she answers Peter's knock on the door.

Peter's first sermon (2:14–41) gives the heart of the

Christian message, and deserves a very careful reading.

In Chapters 9 and 10 are recounted the two main events in the early Christian Church, the conversion of Paul (his pre-conversion name was Saul) and the decision of Peter to baptize the Gentile, Cornelius.

Our Reaction

As we read this book we catch a glimpse of what total dedication to the spirit of the gospel really means. It is not surprising then that the Church throughout the ages has always looked back with a certain nostalgia to the early years described in these pages. The fact that at this critical moment of her history the Church is again discovering the place and the power of the Holy Spirit should be an assurance to all Christians.

PAUL THE MAN

Who Was Paul?

When Jesus was about fifteen years old, Saul (later to be called Paul) was born. His home town was Tarsus, a city situated on the eastern Mediterranean coast of present-day Turkey, some five hundred miles northwards from Nazareth. Today Tarsus is little more than a collection of hovels. Then, it was a magnificent city boasting its own university.

Paul's parents were prosperous citizens and strict Jews. Paul himself was a mixture of three cultures: part Roman, he was later to appeal for justice on the grounds of his Roman citizenship; part Greek, in that this was his everyday language; Jewish by birth and very proud of it. This cosmopolitan background was to stand him in good stead in his missionary work.

We have one description of him which is far from flattering. 'He was a man little of stature, thin-haired, crooked in the legs, with eyebrows joining and nose somewhat hooked, full of grace, for he sometimes appeared like a man, sometimes he had the face of an angel.' While his appearance may have been unprepossessing, his 'presence', his energy, and his openness to whatever the Holy Spirit wanted him to do, was such that he had a greater effect on the development of Christian belief than any other individual in the history of the Church.

The Student

As a boy he was sent to Jerusalem to study the Jewish religion. His tutor was Gamaliel, a Pharisee (see Acts 5:34). (Jesus was still at home in Nazareth at this time.) After five or six years of study he returned to Tarsus to help his father in the tent-making business. But the city of Tarsus was too small for his Jewish religious zeal. Before long he was back in Jerusalem.

We first meet him in Acts at the execution of Stephen. The executioners took off their cloaks and left them 'in the charge of a young man named Saul' (Acts 7:58). 'And Saul approved of his murder.'

The Pharisee
Such was his zeal for the purity of the Jewish religion that he offered his services to hunt out those who believed that Jesus was the Messiah who, having been put to death, was now believed by his followers to be still alive. Later Paul was to write, 'I do not even deserve to be called an apostle, because I persecuted God's church' (I Corinthians 15:9). 'In the meantime Saul kept up his violent threats of murder against the disciples of the Lord. He went to the High Priest and asked for letters of introduction to the Jewish synagogues in Damascus, so that if he should find any followers of the Way of the Lord, he would be able to arrest them, both men and women, and take them back to Jerusalem' (Acts 9:1–2).

Paul Meets Jesus
'On his way to Damascus, as he came near the city, a light from the sky suddenly flashed all around him. He fell to the ground and heard a voice saying to him "Saul, Saul! Why do you persecute me?" "Who are you, Lord?" he asked. "I am Jesus whom you persecute," the voice said' (Acts 9:3–5). This meeting with Jesus is described by Paul five times.* Obviously it is the turning-point of Paul's life. But it is more than that. The words of Jesus identifying himself with the Christians Paul persecutes is the foundation of the doctrine which he is going to preach for the rest of his life: Jesus is to be found in everyone we meet, and we are in Jesus.

* Acts 22, Acts 26, 1 Corinthians 9:1; 15:8; Galatians 1:16.

Paul Meets the Apostles

After regaining his sight (see Acts 9 : 10–18), Paul went
into the Syrian desert to pray. It was a long retreat—two
to three years. At the end of that time he went to
Jerusalem (see Acts 9 : 26–30) to meet the apostles. Paul
must have appeared to the conservatively minded
apostles rather like a newly ordained curate looks in the
eyes of a cautious and elderly parish priest. Their reaction is given in Acts: 'When the brothers [the apostles]
found out about this [a plot to kill him], they took Saul
down to Caesarea and sent him away to Tarsus' (Acts
9 : 30). And there Paul stayed for the next few years.

Come and Help Us

As the years went by, the number of Christians in
Antioch (a beautiful city situated in the country we now
call Syria) increased rapidly. They were nearly all Gentiles. The apostles were able to cope neither with the
numbers nor with the problems peculiar to a situation
outside their experience.

It was fortunate that Barnabas, a colleague of the
apostles, remembered this man whom he had befriended
years before in Jerusalem. 'Then Barnabas went to
Tarsus to look for Saul. When he found him [it was a
city of three hundred thousand people], he brought him
to Antioch. For a whole year the two met with the
people of the church and taught a large group' (Acts
11 : 25). At the end of the year Paul set out on the first
of his three missionary journeys.

Paul the Traveller

Paul was to travel some thirty thousand miles on foot
and more than ten thousand miles by boat. He spent
twenty-two years of his life 'on the road'. Often he
would have to sleep rough. In the country he was in
continual danger from bandits. In the towns his life
was constantly in peril from Jewish religious leaders

who regarded him as a renegade. His health was not good.

Concern for the Churches

In the Second Letter to the Corinthians Paul recalls some of the hardships he has endured for the name of Christ:

> I have worked much harder, I have been in prison more times, I have been whipped much more, and I have been near death more often. Five times I was given the thirty-nine lashes by the Jews; three times I was whipped by the Romans, and once I was stoned; I have been in three shipwrecks, and once I spent twenty-four hours in the water. In my many travels I have been in danger from floods and from robbers, in danger from fellow Jews and from Gentiles; there have been dangers in the cities, dangers in the wilds, dangers in the high seas and dangers from false friends. There has been work and toil; often I have gone without sleep; I have been hungry and thirsty; I have often been without enough food, shelter, or clothing. And, not to mention other things, every day I am under the pressure of my concern for all the churches. (*11:23-8*)

PAUL THE WRITER

Unfair to Paul

It does not do justice to Paul that most Christians hear only snippets from his letters, and these in the detached and often distracting setting of a Sunday service. To appreciate the meaning of these short extracts we should really hear the whole letter, or at least know what it is about. We should know something of the pressing problems that provoked the letter to the local church. Paul did not ask himself, 'Whom shall I write to next?' The circumstances of the people to whom he addressed himself demanded that he write to them, and write quickly.

If we except the epistle to the Christians at Rome, the letters were not painstakingly devised in seclusion. Nor were they written down by Paul himself in such a way that he was able to revise, add or polish. They were dictated in the heat of the moment at a pace that even the most efficient scribe must have found difficult to match. It's true that they form a magnificent compendium of Christian theology, but they are not academic expositions of doctrine. They are charged with emotion and reveal a great deal of their author's sensitive character.

Constant Anxiety

Sometimes the letters are angry and indignant; sometimes tender and loving. Always they breathe the same anxiety he continually felt that the image of Christ be formed in those to whom he had preached.

To see something of Paul's breadth of vision, read his account of the way in which a Christian should love. As you read, picture his secretary, at one time Timothy, later, Silvanus (Silas), using a primitive quill pen on the rough papyrus, labouring to set down each phrase of this stupendous paragraph (I Corinthians 13 : 1–13).

The Problems

Paul was not a haphazard traveller. His itineraries were carefully worked out. In the main he chose those places from which his message was likely to spread, the centres of the trade routes where the highways met and crossed.

Nor was he content simply to establish a church, then to leave it to develop in its own way. He was concerned to revisit the infant Christian communities. If he received news that problems had arisen after his departure, then Paul would tell his secretary to bring papyrus and quill.

We shall see something of the particular problems he wrote about in the introduction to each individual letter. But in the meantime we ought to look at one source of concern to which Paul was frequently forced to refer in his letters.

Judaizers

The first Jewish converts to Christianity could not appreciate that their Jewish beliefs and laws were now superfluous. They wanted the Gentile converts first to accept the Jewish faith, the Jewish law and way of life, and then to believe in Jesus. These 'Judaizers', as they came to be called, dogged Paul's footsteps and tried to win over his converts to circumcision, to a recognition of clean and unclean foods, and the whole complex of Jewish regulations. Even after the matter was settled at the first council in the Church (Acts 15) the difficulties continued. And so to the Galatians Paul wrote, 'You foolish Galatians! . . . How can you be so foolish! You began by God's Spirit; do you now want to finish by your own power?' (Galatians 3 : 1–3.) He describes how he confronted even Peter on this issue (see Galatians 2 : 1–14).

The Law Does Not Save

The Jews had believed that it was the external keeping of
the Law which saved them. This led inevitably to the
self-righteousness of the Pharisees: 'I have kept the Law,
therefore God is obliged to save me.' This is equivalent
to saying, 'I can save myself. I am independent of God.'

This is totally opposed to the Christian spirit. It is not
the Law that saves: it is Christ Jesus who saves us. It is
he who raises us up from our misery. 'Yet we know
that a man is put right with God only through faith in
Jesus Christ, never by doing what the Law requires . . .
If a man is put right with God through the Law, it
means that Christ died for nothing!' (Galatians 2:16,
21.)

Paul was worried that the converts would begin to rely
for salvation on external observances, whereas the power
of Jesus' death-resurrection is the cause of our salvation. It is because of Jesus that there is now 'no difference between Jews and Gentiles, between slaves and free
men, between men and women: you are all one in union
with Christ Jesus' (Galatians 3:28).

In Union with Christ Jesus

This phrase 'in union with Christ Jesus' (or its equivalent) occurs over two hundred times in Paul's letters.
This is the key that opens the door to Paul's thought. In
his Letter to the Romans he writes:

> When we were baptized into union with Christ Jesus,
> we were baptized into union with his death. By our
> baptism, then, we were buried with him and shared
> his death, in order that just as Christ was raised from
> death by the glorious power of the Father, so also we
> might live a new life. For if we became one with him
> in dying as he did, in the same way we shall be one
> with him by being raised to life as he was. (*Romans
> 6:3–5*)

This is the centre of Paul's faith: that Jesus is not just

a hero from the past, nor even one who now lives in some inaccessible place. He is one who lives today, here and now. This was the vision he had received on the road to Damascus. And he applies this belief to every problem. Is there a problem of impurity? How can you join your body, Paul asks, to the body of a prostitute, when you are already 'in Christ Jesus'? Is there a problem of disunity? Where there is dissension, let there be unity because we are all 'in Christ Jesus'. The problem of a runaway slave? 'Now he is not just a slave, but much more than a slave: he is a dear brother in Christ', so please, Philemon, take him back without punishment.

PAUL THE APOSTLE

No Difficulty

When one has to write a difficult letter or compose a written account, one can sometimes sit looking at the sheet of paper for a long time before inspiration comes. It's not easy to begin.

Paul apparently experienced no such difficulty. His ideas and the words that clothed them were not in short supply. Nearly always, in the formal opening sentence of his letters he refers to the fact that he is an apostle. 'From Paul, a servant of Christ Jesus, and an apostle chosen and called by God to preach his Good News' (Romans 1:1). 'From Paul who by the will of God was called to be an apostle . . .' (1 Corinthians 1:1). 'From Paul whose call to be an apostle did not come from man . . . but from Jesus Christ and God the Father, who raised him from death' (Galatians 1:1). 'I am the least of all the apostles—I do not even deserve to be called an apostle, because I persecuted God's church. But by God's grace I am what I am, and the grace that he gave me was not without effect' (1 Corinthians 15:9–10). Paul saw his vocation to be an apostle as totally unified; it was to this that God from all eternity was calling him.

Death – Resurrection

As we have seen, his awareness that Jesus lives on in every Christian dominates his thinking. He is constantly reminding his readers that they are 'in union with Christ Jesus'. But if they are in union with Jesus they are also united to his death and resurrection. This is the paschal mystery in which every Christian shares. In and with Christ we should die to sin, so that in and with Christ we can live for God. There should be in every Christian's life less and less self-seeking, says Paul, and more and more God-seeking. He sees this process as having started at baptism. It is baptism that unites us to Jesus our brother. It unites us to his death–resurrection through which he saves us.

For Paul the whole of the Christian life is nothing more than this progressing death–resurrection, a daily dying to oneself so as to live increasingly for God. 'You are to think of yourselves as dead to sin but alive to God in union with Christ Jesus' (Romans 6:11). This 'dying with Christ' was begun in baptism. Just as he rose to new life so we shall rise because we are in him. And our ability to die daily to ourselves is powered by the Eucharist: 'For until the Lord comes, you proclaim his death whenever you eat this bread and drink from this cup' (I Corinthians, 11:26).

'Until He Comes'

The coming of Jesus Christ is what Paul is continually looking forward to. We are inclined to think of our personal death, the end of our lives, as the terminus of our journey. This was not Paul's view. He sees the ending of a particular human existence as just one stage along the way. 'Until he comes' refers to the coming of our Lord in glory at the end, the finale of this great drama of human existence.

> For just as all men die because of their union to Adam, in the same way all will be raised to life because of their union to Christ. But each one in his proper order: Christ, the first of all; then those who belong to Christ, at the time of his coming. Then the end will come; Christ will overcome all spiritual rulers, authorities and powers and hand over the Kingdom to God the Father. (*I Corinthians 15:22–4*)

When speaking of his own death, he does not expect any immediate reward. The reward he hopes for will be given him 'on that Day'—the Day of the Parousia—

when all God's family will be gathered together in the happiness of heaven.

As for me, the hour has come for me to be sacrificed; the time is here for me to leave this life. I have done my best in the race, I have run the full distance. I have kept the faith. And now the prize of victory is waiting for me, the crown of righteousness which the Lord, the righteous Judge, will give me on that Day—and not only to me, but to all those who wait with love for him to appear. (*2 Timothy 4:8*)

Paul's Death

These are among Paul's last recorded words. They were written from his prison cell in Rome. He had been imprisoned in Rome once before (AD 62) but then he was free to see his friends and, no doubt, celebrate the Eucharist ('the breaking of bread'). His second imprisonment was entirely different. Nero had to find a scapegoat for the great fire which had destroyed most of the city. It was easy for him to stir up the hatred of the mob for those who believed that Jesus alone was the Lord. The persecution of the Christians that followed was savage. It was during this persecution that Paul was imprisoned. Some of his friends deserted him. He felt abandoned. But his concern was not for himself. His anxiety was still for those infant churches he had founded.

We know little about his death. Tradition has it that he was taken outside the city to a place now famous for the basilica of St Paul Outside the Walls. If the usual ceremony of execution was followed, he was first stripped. Then this campaigner for Christ, now weary and old and lonely, was beheaded.

How to Read Paul's Letters

It is first worth noting that the order in which the letters appear in our Bible is not the order in which Paul wrote them. (See pp. 22–3.) Even apart from that, the beginner would best leave the Letter to the Romans (which is given first in the New Testament) till later. Although most scholars would say that this is the greatest of the letters, it is by no means the easiest. It might be best to start with the shortest epistle: the Letter to Philemon. A short introduction to this letter appears on page 140.

The order in which the following introductions appear is the sequence in which most scholars would say the epistles were written. Apart from the Letter to Philemon, this might be the most profitable order in which to read the epistles.

To understand the meaning of each epistle, it is important to know something of the people to whom Paul wrote: their way of life, their way of thinking, the problems that provoked Paul's letter. This we have attempted to describe in each introduction.

In the Gospels, God, our Father, tells us about his Son. He describes the Son he loves in much the same way as any father describes his child to an interested listener: by relating some of the things he did and some of the things he said. In the New Testament letters, the Holy Spirit is inviting us to look again at the *meaning* of the Christian mysteries: the *meaning* of Christ's life and death and resurrection, the *meaning* of baptism, the *meaning* of the Eucharist, the *meaning* of the Church.

TWO LETTERS TO THESSALONIANS

An Ideal Place

Paul, his secretary Silas and companion Timothy arrived in Thessalonica, a town in northern Greece. It was in many respects ideal for Paul's purpose—a trade centre, a port, an administrative capital of a Roman occupied province, with a population of Gentiles and Jews—an ideal place, it would seem to plant the gospel seed. A church would be established and the tiny plant would be tended until itself produced seeds a hundred-fold to be scattered along the criss-cross of trade routes.

According to his usual habit, Paul went to the synagogue. There during three Sabbath days he argued with the people from the Scriptures, explaining them and proving from them that the Messiah had to suffer and be raised from death . . . Some of them were convinced and joined Paul and Silas; so did a large group of Greeks who worshipped God, and many of the leading women.

But the Jews were jealous and gathered some of the worthless loafers from the street and formed a mob . . . They set the whole city in an uproar . . . (See *Acts 17:2–5*)

Paul was forced to leave. He escaped to Berea, a town some fifty miles away. Hardly had he here begun to attract converts before the agitators from Thessalonica arrived and again made it impossible for Paul to stay. 'At once the brothers sent Paul away to the coast, but both Silas and Timothy stayed in Berea. The men who were taking Paul went with him as far as Athens. Then they went back to Berea with instructions from Paul that Silas and Timothy join him as soon as possible' (Acts 17:14–15).

The Reunion
But Timothy alone arrived in Athens with the sad news
that Paul's absence had not lessened the violence of the
Thessalonian mobs against his converts. All Paul could
do was to ask Timothy to return to Thessalonica to find
out at first hand how the infant church there would stand
up to continuing persecution.

At the same time Paul's sermons to the cynics of
Athens were meeting with shrugs and smiles. He was a
failure. In a state of despondency he made the forty-
mile overland journey to another Greek town, Corinth.
Here he waited impatiently for the news of Thessalonica
that he knew Timothy and Silas would soon bring.
Would the faith of his converts be able to withstand the
pressure of persecution? The reunion of the three of
them was made the happier by the news that, despite
their trials, the Christian Thessalonians had stood firm.

Our Pride and Joy
This then was the occasion of the first two letters (in
the New Testament) that Paul wrote.* The relief and joy
at the welcome news Timothy brought is apparent. 'We
always thank God for you all, and always mention you in
our prayers. For we remember before our God and
Father . . . how your hope in our Lord Jesus Christ is
firm' (1 Thessalonians 1 : 2–3). 'Indeed you are our pride
and joy' (1 Thessalonians 2 : 20).

The two letters were written within months of each
other around about the year AD 50. Many Christians of
this time (and for a while even the apostles themselves)
believed that the Parousia, the coming of our Lord at the
end of the world, was imminent. So imminent, in fact,
that some of them saw no point in working. Why bother
to work when the end was so near? (Even in our day it is
not unknown for groups of people to forecast a forth-

* The letters of Paul do not appear in our Bibles in the order
in which they were written.

coming date for the end of the world and behave in much the same way.) Paul had to disabuse his readers of the idea that the Christian could opt out of daily affairs. Even so, Paul does not deny that the coming of the Lord may take place in their own life time. In his second letter he modifies this teaching.

His Message for Us

Of course there are other things that Paul writes about in these two letters: the close presence of God, the fact that our salvation consists in our being united to Jesus by faith. The mystery of the Church, the necessity for fraternal charity. We also catch more than a glimpse of Paul's character, his warmth, his feeling of involvement with the flock he had gathered together.

However, as we read these two letters, we may well be led to reflect on the coming in glory of Jesus. This is what we pray for when we say 'Thy Kingdom come,' 'I look forward to the resurrection of the dead and the life of the world to come'.

THE FIRST LETTER TO
THE CORINTHIANS

We have seen something of the events that preceded Paul's stay in Corinth (see pp. 117–18): his expulsion from Thessalonica and Berea, his failure at Athens followed by his happy reunion with Silas and Timothy in Corinth. You can read (in Acts 18) of Paul's efforts to build a community in Corinth. After labouring there for a year and a half he left Greece and made for Ephesus, then a bustling port, now a cluster of ruins on the coast of Turkey.

The Background
To understand the two letters to the Corinthians we must know something of the people to whom he wrote.

Corinth was a city of some half a million souls: merchants and dockers, Jews and Gentiles, sailors and slaves (of the total population some 200,000 were slaves). Side by side with strict Jewish religious practice flourished the grossest sexual vices, often associated with the worship of pagan deities. Temple prostitution was accepted as a respectable occupation, a normal accompaniment to pagan worship. The reputation of the city was well known. 'A Corinthian girl' meant only one thing. 'To live like a Corinthian' was a polite expression used to describe a life of debauchery.

In this city there was little of the openness and joy to be found in other more rural communities of Asia Minor. In Corinth the desire for a quick profit at the expense of others was as much a part of life as the fresh sea air blowing in from the Aegean. It was among people living in such depraved surroundings that Paul founded one of his most flourishing communities. Nevertheless it is not surprising that granted such a background he had later to address some hard words of correction to the Corinthians.

Disturbing News

Once settled in his next mission, Ephesus, Paul busied himself with preaching and teaching. But news soon came to him that all was not well with his converts at Corinth. Paul wrote to them. Unfortunately this first letter is lost. Paul refers to it in our First Letter to the Corinthians: 'In the letter that I wrote you . . .' (5:9). His second letter (our first) is Paul's answer to various problems put to him by the Christians of Corinth. In addition he seeks to rectify irregularities in the church there, of which he had heard rumours. The people of Corinth must have been surprised to receive in reply, not only solutions to the questions they had asked, but a severe rebuke for things they believed Paul knew nothing about.

Divisions in the Church (Chapters 1–6)

Paul deals with these irregularities in the first six chapters. His chief anxiety is for the unity of the Church. 'Agree, all of you, in what you say, so there will be no divisions among you' (1:10). He has heard, too, that some of his converts are succumbing to their old ways. 'Now it is actually being said that there is sexual immorality among you so terrible that not even the heathen would be guilty of it' (5:1). In addition, some of the Christians are so envious of each other that they are settling their disputes before the pagan courts. 'If one of you has a dispute with a brother, how dare he go before heathen judges, instead of letting God's people settle the matter?' (6:1)

Answers to Questions (Chapters 7–10)

The questions Paul was asked concerned marriage and virginity and Paul answers them in Chapter 7. Then he deals with a question that may seem remote to our situation, but it was real enough to the housewife of Corinth who wanted to buy food that had been sacrificed to idols. Paul's solution, however, has implications which do concern us today. 'Be careful . . . and do not let your freedom of action make those who are weak in faith fall into sin' (8:9).

The Celebration of the Eucharist (Chapters 11–14)

The early Christian families met in each other's houses to celebrate the Eucharist. Certain abuses had sprung up. 'When you meet together as a group, you do not come to eat the Lord's Supper. For as you eat, each one goes ahead with his own meal, so that some are hungry while others get drunk' (11:17–21).

Paul's remarks on the place of women in the liturgical assembly may not evoke much sympathy today unless we keep in mind the attitude to women prevalent in his day.

At these assemblies, individuals were 'possessed by the Spirit': some received the gift (charism) of miracles, some the charism of speaking, some that of discernment, and so on. Paul is at pains to point out that these gifts count for nothing if they do not serve the cause of love. 'I may be able to speak the languages of men and even of angels, but if I have not love, my speech is no more than a noisy gong or a clanging bell' (13:1).

The Resurrection of the Dead (Chapter 15)

Many of his converts at Corinth were Greek, and the Greeks found the doctrine of the resurrection of the body (which we confess in the Apostles' Creed) particularly difficult to believe. Paul begins with the resurrection of Christ's body. 'Now, since our message is that Christ has been raised from death, how can some of you say that the dead will not be raised to life? If that is true, it means that Christ was not raised; and if Christ has not been raised from death, then we have nothing to preach, and you have nothing to believe' (15:12).

Then he goes on to declare that, because we are one with Christ, we too will be raised just as he was.

For just as all men die because of their union to Adam, in the same way all will be raised to life because of their union to Christ. But each one in his proper order: Christ the first of all; then those who belong to Christ, at the time of his coming. Then the end will come; Christ will overcome all spiritual rulers, authorities and powers, and hand over the Kingdom to God the Father. (*15:22–4*)

The Message for Us

A brief outline of the letter's structure as given above does little justice to Paul. For the apostle does much more than answer questions. He gives us a vision of the unity of the Church—the body of Christ—in which all are invited to use their talents (Chapters 12 and 13). He speaks of immorality in terms, not of impersonal law-breaking, but as an affront to the personal relationship between the Christian and Christ (Chapter 6). He reminds his readers that the Eucharist is a celebration of unity: it would be a total perversion of Christ's intention if it should become an occasion of division within the Church (Chapters 10 and 11). His words are as relevant to the Christian of today as they were to the hard-pressed converts of Corinth in AD 57.

THE LETTER TO THE GALATIANS

Setting the Scene

To understand something of the anxiety Paul felt as he dictated this fiery letter, we might think of the following imaginary situation: a bishop of today is forced, for various extrinsic reasons, to leave his diocese for some considerable time. He has done his best as the pastor of his flock to lead his people into an awareness of the vision put forward by Vatican II. After careful instruction, all the reforms asked for by the Council are in course of being carried out.

In his absence, however, a group of influential people begin to undermine his authority and try to reverse these reforms. 'Let's go back to the pre-Council days', they say. 'Our bishop doesn't know what he's talking about. He's not a real bishop. He's just an innovator.'

Many of the ordinary folk of the diocese are confused. Some wish to return to the old ways. Others are undecided. Most are beginning to become a little suspicious of the authority and wisdom of their absent pastor. Eventually the bishop hears of this sad state of affairs. He sends for his secretary and dictates a vehement pastoral letter which he orders to be read in all churches of his diocese the following Sunday.

Circumcision or Baptism

The people to whom Paul wrote his letter were in danger of being persuaded to adopt a much more retrograde faith and practice than is imagined in the above example. The Judaizers (we have met them more than once already; see pp. 110–11) were saying that Gentiles could be saved only if they first became Jews: that before convert Gentiles could be baptized they must first submit to Jewish circumcision and Jewish law and Jewish ritual. They were saying that Paul was not a genuine apostle; he had not lived with Jesus as had the other apostles. He was a heretic. They alone were orthodox believers.

His Credentials

Paul wastes little time on the preliminary courtesies customary at the start of a letter. He makes his position clear immediately:

> From Paul, whose call to be an apostle did not come from man or by means of man, but from Jesus Christ and God the Father, who raised him from death. (*1:1*)
>
> I am surprised at you! In no time at all you are deserting the one who called you by the grace of Christ, and are going to another gospel . . . We have said it before, and now I say it again: if anyone preaches to you a gospel that is different from the one you accepted, may he be condemned to hell! (*1: 6, 9*)

Paul's argument is this: it is not the keeping of the commandments (and all the other laws) that saves a person. A man is saved only because he is in union with Christ Jesus. In other words we do not keep the commandments in order to be saved. That would imply that we can achieve salvation by our own efforts. We are saved through being united to Jesus (through baptism, not circumcision) and it is because we are united to him that we keep the commandments. Since we are 'a new creation in Christ Jesus', there is now 'no difference between Jews and Gentiles'. None of the other prescriptions of the Jewish faith (the kosher foods, the purifications etc.) can therefore be of obligation.

The Message for Today

As you read this short letter you cannot fail to notice the emotional tone of the writing. No one likes to be accused of heresy!

But there is more to it than that. Paul saw in the action of the Judaizers the danger of the Church losing its own identity. The crisis was that faith in the Law would replace faith in Jesus. Facing the real possibility of such a catastrophic reversal of the gospel message, could Paul be expected to write calmly and temperately?

The passage about Hagar and Sarah (4:21–31) would be appreciated by the Galatians of the first century. The argument speaks less directly to us today.

Apart from those few verses, the message of this letter is clear enough for Christians of the twentieth century.

THE SECOND LETTER TO
THE CORINTHIANS

The Background

The circumstances of the First Letter to the Corinthians are clear enough (see pp. 120ff). The events surrounding the writing of 2 Corinthians are less certain. A likely reconstruction is as follows:

After writing 1 Corinthians, Paul made the short voyage from Ephesus to Corinth in order to reinforce the instructions he had given by letter. During this visit some sort of confrontation with a member of the congregation caused him great sadness and Paul was forced, after leaving Corinth, to dictate another stern letter—'For this is the reason I wrote you *that letter*: I wanted to find out how well you had stood the test, and whether you are always ready to obey my instructions' (2 Corinthians 2:9—authors' italics). Unfortunately this letter, like the very first one Paul wrote to the Corinthians, is lost.

Better News

Back at Ephesus again, Paul ran into further trouble. You can read about this in Acts (Chapter 19). 'The burdens laid upon us were so great and so heavy, that we gave up all hope of living. We felt that the sentence of death had been passed against us. But this happened so that we should rely, not upon ourselves but only on God, who raised the dead' (2 Corinthians 1:8–9).

The riot in Ephesus was attributed to Paul and once again he was forced to flee.

He journeyed back to Greece, probably to Philippi. There he met Titus who had just come from Corinth with the good news that Paul's severe letter (the one that is lost) had achieved its purpose: the Corinthians were reconciled to each other and to Paul.

> Even after we arrived in Macedonia [possibly Philippi] we did not have any rest. There were troubles everywhere, quarrels with others, fears in our hearts. But God, who encourages the downhearted, encouraged us with the coming of Titus. It was not only his coming, but also his report of how you encouraged him. He told us how much you want to see me, how sorry you are, how ready you are to defend me; and so I am even happier now. (*2 Corinthians 7:5–7*)

Apologia

And so it was with relief that Paul wrote this next letter to his flock at Corinth. Nevertheless he is at pains, even now, to assert his authority as an apostle. The first seven and the last three chapters are devoted to an apologia for his actions. Sandwiched in between are two chapters (8–9) in which he appeals for a collection he is making. His fund is for the Christians in Jerusalem. The persecution of the church there had left the Christians penniless. Paul appeals to the converts of the comparatively prosperous people of Corinth.

This letter is not easy to read. One moment Paul's tenderness and love is apparent. At another, he appears severe and unyielding. One possible cause of this changing pattern may be that Paul did not dictate the letter at one sitting. We can be fairly sure that his dictation suffered from interruptions. Even so 2 Corinthians, in presenting as it does a highly personal description of Paul's own apostolate (especially its difficulties) offers something of a mandate to all those who would aspire to be apostles today.

THE LETTER TO THE ROMANS

The Background
A German scholar has said that this letter to the Christians at Rome would have required ninety-eight hours of dictation. It is the longest of Paul's letters and he worked at it on and off during the winter of AD 57–58.

We have seen that most of Paul's letters were written in the heat of the moment, usually to answer difficulties or settle disputes in the churches that he had founded. This letter was different. He was not writing to Christians of a church he had founded or even visited. Nor was he writing to settle problems—although he deals with the perennial difficulty of the relationship between Judaism and Christianity. It seems rather that Paul was writing this letter in preparation for his proposed visit to Rome.

A Controversial Figure
As we have seen (in the introduction to Galatians) Paul was regarded as a near-heretic by the Judaizers. To the Romans he may well have appeared to be something almost as bad, 'a controversial figure'. So in this pre-visit document Paul is at pains to set out clearly his Christian belief. The message he had sent to the Galatians, composed part angrily, part sadly, he now repeats and expands for the Christians of Rome, but in calm and measured prose. It is more a closely argued exposition than a letter. If we were to give this treatise a title, 'What it means to be a Christian' would sum it up.

A State of Sin
Paul wrote this letter from Corinth. As we have seen elsewhere (see pp. 120 ff.), Corinth was one of the most

depraved places on earth. Temple prostitution, sexual orgies and perversions, the whole pitiless and remorseless fabric of a life lived without God were in evidence about him. It is hardly any wonder then that he should use this depravity as an argument for man's need of a saviour.

> Because of what men do, God has given them over to shameful passions. Even the women pervert the natural use of their sex by unnatural acts. In the same way the men give up natural sexual relations with women and burn with passion for each other . . . Because men refuse to keep in mind the true knowledge about God, he has given them over to corrupted minds, so that they do the things they should not. They are filled with all kinds of wickedness, evil, greed, and vice; they are full of jealousy, murder, fighting, deceit, and malice. They gossip, and speak evil of one another; they are hateful to God, insolent, proud, and boastful . . . they show no kindness or pity to others. *(1:28–31)*

A Saviour

Then Paul turns to the Jews among his readers (2:17). He tells them that they have no cause for pride. The Law they admire is no saviour. God himself sent the Jews a saviour in the person of Jesus Christ. But the Jews refused to believe in Jesus and for this reason they forfeited their status as the chosen people of God. They believed that they were saved because of what they themselves did. Whereas in fact we are saved because of what God has done for us. 'His [God's] choice is based on his mercy, not on what they [men] have done. For if God's choice were based on what men do, then his mercy would not be true mercy' (11:6).

The Contrast

In the opening chapter Paul painted the horrifying picture of a life lived without God. In Chapters 5, 6 and 8 he describes the life of one who tries to live 'in union with Christ Jesus' by the power of the Holy Spirit. These chapters radiate joy and hope. They are the very heart of Paul's message.

> Christ Jesus is the one who died, or rather, who was raised to life and is at the right side of God. He pleads with God for us! Who, then, can separate us from the love of Christ? Can trouble do it, or hardship, or persecution, or hunger, or poverty, or danger, or death? . . . No, in all these things we have complete victory through him who loved us! For I am certain that nothing can separate us from his love: neither death nor life; neither angels nor other heavenly rulers or powers; neither the present nor the future; neither the world above nor the world below—there is nothing in all creation that will ever be able to separate us from the love of God which is ours through Christ Jesus, our Lord. (8:34–9)

Where to Begin

The Letter to the Romans is the greatest of all Paul's epistles. A whole library could be built around the hundreds of commentaries that have been devoted solely to this work. It is not easy to read.

It might be best to start with the chapters (5, 6 and 8) mentioned above. Then turn to Chapter 12 and see how frequently you catch here the echo of Christ's words recorded in the Gospels.

Having read his letter, the Christians of Rome must have looked forward to Paul's arrival. The churches he had established in the East were thriving. Paul had begun to look to the West.

> Now that I have finished my work in these [eastern] regions, and since I have been wanting for so many years to come to see you, I hope to do so now. I would like to see you on my way to Spain, and be helped by you to go there, after I have enjoyed visiting you for a

while. Right now, however, I am going to Jerusalem
. . . Pray that I may be kept safe from the unbelievers
in Judea, and that my service in Jerusalem may be
acceptable to God's people there. And so I will come
to you full of joy, if it is God's will, and enjoy a re-
freshing visit with you *(15:23–31)*

But it was not God's will. Paul was arrested in Jerusalem
and arrived in Rome, late by some three years, and a
prisoner of the Roman Emperor.

THE LETTER TO THE PHILIPPIANS

The Background

Paul wrote this letter from prison. Although there is some dispute about where precisely he was imprisoned when he wrote; the traditional view is that he was in a Roman gaol as he dictated (in the year 62 or 63) this short 'thank you' note to his friends at Philippi.

The town of Philippi is in the north of Greece. Paul had visited it three times in the years 50, 57 and 58. If you read Acts 16, you will see what happened to him on his first visit. He knew his converts well and loved them all. And they loved him. When they heard that he was in prison, they made a collection for him. One of their number, Epaphroditus, was entrusted to make the six-week journey to Rome to present this gift personally to him. The Letter to the Philippians is Paul's message of gratitude sent back with Epaphroditus. 'I have thought it necessary to send you our brother Epaphroditus, who has worked and fought by my side, and who has served as your messenger in helping me. He is anxious to see you all, and is very upset because you heard that he was sick. Indeed he was sick, and almost died—but God had pity on him; and not only on him but on me, too, and spared me even greater sorrow' (2:25–7).

The Message

The whole letter breathes joy and serenity. Despite his imprisonment Paul is happy because he realizes that his living relationship with the risen Christ Jesus outweighs all the sufferings that men can inflict.

The most famous passage of this short letter is contained in Chapter 2, verses 6 to 11. These verses may well have been taken from one of the early Christian hymns. They describe the humility of the Son of God in renouncing his right to glory in order to become a member of the fallen human race and this so that he might become the servant of all.

Later in the letter (3:4–11) Paul describes some of the privileges of a Pharisee he has renounced in order to serve Christ and the Christian family. 'For his sake I have thrown everything away; I consider it all as mere garbage, so that I might gain Christ and be completely united with him' (3:8).

Good News

The literal meaning of 'gospel' is 'good news', and good news brings joy. That word 'joy' appears twelve times in this short letter.

Joy does not exclude the possibility of suffering. And Christians over the centuries have gained from the Letter to the Philippians comfort and courage in the trials they have suffered for their faith. Like Paul, they too have found 'the strength to face all conditions by the power that Christ gives me' (4:13).

THE LETTER TO THE COLOSSIANS

An Insignificant Town
You will look in vain for the town of Colossae in any atlas of contemporary place names. It no longer exists. It was situated about a hundred miles east of Ephesus. That puts it somewhere in the middle of present-day Turkey.

Despite its grandiose name, it was an insignificant town. Paul had never visited it personally. He had, however, visited and preached in Ephesus several times. Possibly some Colossians in visiting Ephesus had heard Paul preach and in this way taken the Christian faith back to their home town. It is certainly likely that Epaphras, the leader of the church at Colossae, had met Paul at Ephesus and had been commissioned by him to be the bishop, the *episcopus* (from the Greek word meaning 'overseer'), of the Christian community there.

The Background
Perhaps it was that Epaphras wrote to Paul in prison (probably in Rome) and told him that all was not well with the Christians at Colossae. They had begun to borrow some of the ideas that properly belonged to local pagan religions. They were beginning to interweave these notions with the Christian message. For one thing they had begun to lose sight of the fact that Jesus is the one mediator between God and men. Instead they believed that God was so remote (in their view) from this totally evil world as to make it necessary for a whole hierarchy of angels or spiritual powers to act as intermediaries. Christ was high up in this hierarchy but by no means was he supreme. Perhaps the Christian faith was too simple, too straightforward, for the Colossians, for they

were also beginning to make for themselves additional prescriptions. 'Why do you obey such rules as "Don't handle this," "Don't taste that," "Don't touch the other"?' (2:21) Paul wrote to them.

The Truth

Paul is at pains in the letter he sent back with Tychicus (together with the Letter to Philemon about the slave Onesimus) to remind the Colossians of the true Christian faith. Christ is not one mediator among many.

> Christ is the visible likeness of the invisible God. He is the first-born Son, superior to all created things. For by him God created everything in heaven and on earth, the seen and the unseen things, including spiritual powers, lords, rulers, and authorities. God created the whole universe through him and for him. He existed before all things and in union with him all things have their proper place. He is the head of his body, the church; he is the source of the body's life; he is the first-born Son who was raised from death, in order that he alone might have the first place in all things. (*1:15–18*)

Happy Fault

No doubt the Colossians were at fault in trying to embellish and so distort the Christian message with alien ideas. But it was a 'happy fault' in that it provoked Paul into setting out so clearly the supreme centrality of Christ. It may well be that the difficulties of these people forced Paul to look again at his own understanding of Christ's place in the universe. For when one compares this letter with epistles Paul had written ten or so years earlier, one sees a real advance in his understanding. Paul speaks of the 'mystery of Christ', not the 'fact of Christ'. A fact is something a person can master once and for all. A mystery is something that one appreciates and understands more fully as time goes by. If this is true of Paul's understanding of Christ, how much more so should it be the experience of the ordinary Christian who, in his thoughts and prayers and reading, daily seeks to enter more and more into the mind of Christ.

THE LETTER TO THE EPHESIANS

The Background

Although some scholars would dispute Paul's authorship
of Ephesians, the traditional view is that this is yet
another letter dictated by Paul during his first imprisonment in Rome (AD 60–3). In much the same way that his
Letter to the Romans was an elaboration of the message
he had sent to the Galatians, so this Letter to the Ephesians is an expansion of the subject matter contained in
his Letter to the Colossians—the supreme centrality of
Christ in whom we are all united.

Most of Paul's letters contained detailed references and
goodwill messages to individuals mentioned by name.
Because there are no such topical allusions in Ephesians,
it is thought that this letter was addressed to a far wider
audience. It is more in the nature of an encyclical letter
intended possibly for all the churches in Asia Minor.

The Message

Paul was now serving a prison sentence in Rome because
he had been arrested in Jerusalem five years previously.
The occasion of his arrest was the uproar caused when
he took a Gentile, Trophimus, to the other side of the
wall of the Temple precinct beyond which no non-Jew
was allowed (see Acts 21:27ff). In this letter (1:10–11)
he describes the whole sweep of God's mighty plan in
giving men his own Son so that all creatures would be
united in him. 'For Christ himself has brought us peace,
by making the Jews and Gentiles one people. With his
own body he *broke down the wall* that separated them
and kept them enemies (2:14—authors' italics). He
further develops this imagery: 'You, too, are built upon
the foundation laid by the apostles and prophets, the

cornerstone being Christ Jesus himself. He is the one who holds the whole building together and makes it grow into a sacred temple in the Lord' (2:20–1).

The Content

In the first three chapters, Paul deals with Christian *belief*: God's plan for men, the reconciliation of Jew and Gentile, Paul's own commission to preach to the Gentiles.

In the last three chapters he deals with Christian *behaviour*: the need for unity, the necessity of breaking with pagan practices, and of Christ-like conduct in a Christian home.

It is likely that Paul's guard was a Roman soldier. Possibly the armour worn by his guard inspired the last few lines of his letter:

> So take up God's armour now! . . . Have truth for a belt tight round your waist; put on righteousness for your breastplate, and the readiness to announce the Good News of peace as shoes for your feet. At all times carry faith as a shield . . . And accept salvation for a helmet, and the word of God as the sword that the Spirit gives you. *(6:13–17)*

THE LETTER TO PHILEMON

The Background

'From Paul, a prisoner for the sake of Christ Jesus, and from our brother Timothy—To our friend and fellow worker Philemon' (verse 1). This, the shortest of Paul's letters, is entirely personal. It is directed to one individual, Philemon, a pillar of the church at Colossae. It concerns itself solely with the fate of another individual, Onesimus.

Onesimus was a runaway slave and as such was liable to severe punishment. He was not only a convert of Paul's but had become his active helper. Paul writes from prison to Philemon and asks that Onesimus be accepted back, not simply without punishment, but with love and kindness, 'as a brother in the Lord' (verse 16).

Paul does not inveigh against slavery. Rather, he gently points out that all Christians, slave or free, are true brothers in Christ. How can my brother be my slave? This is the question Paul leaves Philemon to put to himself.

LETTERS TO TITUS AND
TIMOTHY

The Background
The three letters, one to Titus and two to Timothy are
called 'the Pastoral Epistles'. A bishop is called the
pastor of his flock and these three letters are addressed
to bishops. After Paul had been released from prison, he
appointed Titus Bishop of Crete and Timothy Bishop
of Ephesus. In these letters Paul sends a message of encouragement to his two close friends and co-workers.
The Acts of the Apostles ends with Paul's first imprisonment in Rome (from where it is likely Paul wrote
letters to the Philippians, to Philemon, to the Colossians,
and to the Ephesians). We know very little of Paul's
movements after his release. We can be sure however
that he soon set out from Rome to revisit the churches
he had founded. Tradition has it that he even went as
far as Spain.

The Message
Obviously Paul intended the pastoral letters to reach a
wider audience than Timothy and Titus. In fact they
have been described as 'open letters to all preachers of
the gospel'. He is no longer concerned to set forth any
further development of his understanding of the Christian message. His chief concern is that his converts
should hold fast to the faith they have received.

I command you to preach the message, to insist upon
telling it, whether the time is right or not; to con-
vince, reproach and encourage, teaching with all
patience. For the time will come when men will not
listen to true teaching, but will follow their own desires, and will collect for themselves more and more

teachers who will tell them what they are itching to hear. (*2 Timothy 4:1–3*)

Hold to the true words that I taught you, as the example for you to follow and stay in the faith and love that are ours in union with Christ Jesus. (*2 Timothy 1:13*)

Last Will and Testament

Some scholars are doubtful whether in fact Paul was the author of the Pastoral Epistles. They say that they were edited by his disciples some considerable time after his death. This is only a supposition and it is hard to see how it could ever be proved.

On the other hand, when one reads 2 Timothy, one cannot but be moved by the sense of impending death. For if the traditional view is accepted then this letter was dictated by Paul when he was incarcerated below ground in the dark and damp Mamertine gaol of Rome. How different from the 'house arrest' of his first imprisonment! The great fire of Rome which had destroyed almost the whole of the city was blamed upon the Christians. Anyone gaoled now had little chance of release.

This last letter has the character of a last will and testament. Many of his friends have deserted him and he begs Timothy to come to him and bring his coat and parchments. 'Do your best to come to me soon' (4:9), and a few lines further on, 'Do your best to come before winter' (4:21).

As for me, the hour has come for me to be sacrificed; the time is here for me to leave this life. I have done my best in the race, I have run the full distance, I have kept the faith. And now the prize of victory is waiting for me, the crown of righteousness which the Lord, the righteous Judge, will give me on that Day —and not only to me, but to all those who wait with love for him to appear. (*4: 6–8*)

THE LETTER TO THE HEBREWS

The Background

It ought to be said at the outset that we know very little about the background to Hebrews. We know neither who wrote it nor for whom it was intended. If you have read some of Paul's letters you will notice right away that the style of Hebrews is quite different.

Hardly anyone would say that Paul was the author. The writer may have been one of Paul's disciples for it contains many Pauline ideas. For example, the fact of Jesus as the one mediator between God and men is the main theme, and this was a topic to which Paul constantly returned.

Our Priest

But the writer goes further in his description of Christ as our mediator with the Father: he is a *priest-mediator* who through the sacrifice of his own life earned salvation for those who are united to him in faith. '[Jesus] had to become like his brothers in every way, in order to be their faithful and merciful high priest in his service to God, so that the people's sins would be forgiven. And now he can help those who are tempted, because he himself was tempted and suffered' (2:17-18). Jesus' priesthood did not come to an end with his sacrificial death. 'Jesus lives on for ever, and his work as priest does not pass on to someone else. And so he is able, now and always, to save those who come to God through him, because he lives for ever to plead with God for them' (7:24-5).

How to Read Hebrews

We know that 'a great number' of the Temple priests

had become Christians (Acts 6:7). Their work of butchering lambs in the Temple precinct was at an end once their faith in Jesus' self-sacrifice as the Lamb of God made all other sacrifices superfluous. Some scholars have tentatively suggested that Hebrews may have been written in order to encourage and console such a group as this.

However, the letter was intended to be read by Gentiles as well as Jews. Even so, it presumes an acquaintance with the Old Testament that is perhaps lacking among many Christians today. For this reason, it might be best to start with the very core of the work—4:14 to 5:10. Here the writer speaks with great tenderness of the continuing work of 'Our great high priest . . . who was tempted in every way that we are, but did not sin' (4:15).

THE LETTER FROM JAMES

Who Is James?

There are a number of 'James's' in the New Testament. One is the son of Zebedee, the brother of John. He was executed by Herod in AD 42.

A second James is another apostle, the son of Alphaeus.

A third James is described in the Gospels as 'the brother [i.e. kinsman] of the Lord'. He became the leader of the Christian community in Jerusalem. Paul described him as a 'pillar of the church'. He played a significant part in the deliberations of the First Council in deciding that Gentile converts should not be obliged to adopt Jewish practices. (See Acts 15:13–23.) It is generally agreed that this third James is the author of the letter. If such is the case, then this epistle must have been written about the middle of the first century and is thus one of the earliest of all Christian writings.

The Message

If you have read some of Paul's letters, one thing will strike you immediately after reading the Letter from James: the absence of almost all reference to the place and person of Jesus. Perhaps this can be explained by the fact that if the letter were written so early, difficulties and debates about the role of Christ in our salvation had not yet arisen.

There can be no doubt however that it is the work of a man who is steeped in the teaching of Jesus, whose sayings are echoed in many passages.

A Picture of Today

James concentrates not so much on doctrine as on behaviour. The trials of being a Christian in a non-Christian society, the temptation to adopt the non-Christian standards of society, the quarrelling and dissension prevalent amongst Christians, the danger of paying more attention to the rich and influential than to the poor—those are the subjects about which James writes. A picture of the early Christian community emerges from this letter and it is a picture in which we might recognize ourselves today.

THE FIRST LETTER FROM PETER

The Background
'I write you this brief letter with the help of Silvanus . . .'
(5:12). So Peter humbly concludes his letter written from
Rome (the pseudonym for Rome was 'Babylon', 5:13)
to the Christians dispersed throughout Asia Minor. As
we have seen (p. 109), Silvanus was Paul's secretary for a
time. His experience as a scribe could well be the
answer to the question: how could a simple, unlettered,
fisherman of Galilee write such excellent Greek?

Peter wrote this letter—the first papal encyclical—
just three or four years before his death in AD 67. It is
believed that much of it is taken from the sermon he was
in the habit of giving before baptizing his converts. It
could be that Silvanus not only reproduced his master's
homily, but, with Peter's approval, added to it. We
should not be surprised, then, if throughout the five short
chapters of this letter we hear the echo of some of the
phrases Silvanus had written down at Paul's dictation.

The Content
Peter's letter is written to encourage Christians in time
of trial. Not yet, it is believed, the trial of a savage persecution—that was to come later. But rather the trials
any Christian experiences while trying to live in a pagan
society. 'My dear friends, do not be surprised at the pain-
ful test you are suffering, as though something unusual
were happening to you. Rather be glad that you are
sharing Christ's sufferings, so that you may be full of
joy when his glory is revealed' (4:12–13).

In order to give the apostles a living example of service, Jesus 'took off his outer garment, and tied a towel
round his waist' (John 13:4). He attempted to wash

Peter's feet first. Is Peter recalling this scene when he writes, 'All of you must put on the apron of humility to serve one another' (5:5)?

The Message

It is not easy to live a Christian life in a post-Christian world. Christians dispersed throughout the world today are increasingly isolated as they attempt to live according to the gospel. They cannot rely on the sympathetic outlook of a Christian society. Peter's words written nearly two thousand years ago have a remarkable relevance to our own age.

THE SECOND LETTER FROM PETER

The Background

From the beginning, doubts have been expressed as to whether Peter was in fact the author of this letter. But this doubt does not need to worry us. It was an accepted practice for an unknown author to borrow the name of someone better known in order to lend weight to his words. The Second Letter from Peter belongs to a body of writings for which the Church guaranteed the inspiration of the Holy Spirit. Even if Peter were not the author, we can be sure that the words faithfully reflect his mind.

The Content

The message of 2 Peter is similar to that contained in the Letter from Jude. God has given us salvation through his Son, Jesus, whose coming we await. We must not be deceived by false teachers. 'These men are like dried-up springs, like clouds blown along by a storm . . . They make proud and stupid statements, and use immoral bodily lusts to trap those who are just barely escaping from among people who live in error. They promise them freedom, while they themselves are slaves of destructive habits . . .' (2:17–19). 'Your lives should be holy and dedicated to God, as you wait for the Day of God . . . And so, my friends, as you wait for that Day, do your best to be pure and faultless in God's sight and to be at peace with him' (3:11–14).

It is generally believed that Jude is the brother of James (the author of another letter in the New Testament, and the 'brother [kinsman] of the Lord'). The Letter from Jude may well have been composed after James's execution.

Jude warns his readers against those who would pervert the gospel as handed down from the apostles. It is addressed not to any particular group but rather to Christians in general. There are hints that this perversion is not so much a distortion of Christian belief but rather of behaviour. It could be that some converts wrongly confused the freedom of the gospel with an immoral permissiveness.

THE FIRST LETTER OF JOHN

The Background

As we have seen (p. 95), John wrote his Gospel so that people would believe in Jesus as the Son of God. This letter of John's, perhaps written shortly after his Gospel, has a different purpose. It is addressed to those who already believe: 'I write you this so that you may know that you have eternal life—you who believe in the name of the Son of God' (5:13).

The first deviation from the gospel of Jesus Christ, the first heresy, was Gnosticism. The word *gnosis* is Greek for 'knowledge'.

A number of Christians were beginning to embellish their faith with alien ideas drawn from the pagan environment in which they lived. They were in danger of becoming Gnostics. Gnostics believed that they were saved, liberated, from this world (which they believed to be totally evil), by a special system of knowledge. Because the material of this world was so evil, they could not bring themselves to believe that Jesus was truly human. The possession of this knowledge also led the Gnostics to think that they belonged to a special group, superior to the community of the Church. They believed also that the knowledge to which they alone had access absolved them from the obligation of keeping the commandments.

The Content

Many scholars believe that John wrote this first letter—an encyclical addressed to Christians in general—with the purpose of combating this heresy. ('I write you this about those who are trying to deceive you' 2:26.) For he emphasizes the reality of Jesus, the Word of God made flesh, whom he had seen and touched (1:1). He says that we *can* sin, 'but if anyone does sin, we have Jesus Christ, the righteous, who pleads for us with the Father' (2:1). He speaks frequently of the commandments and, in particular, the one commandment which not only contains all the others but keeps the Christian community united:

> We love because God first loved us. If someone says, 'I love God,' yet hates his brother, he is a liar. For he cannot love God, whom he has not seen, if he does not love his brother, whom he has seen. This, then, is the command that God gave us: he who loves God must love his brother also. (*4:19–21*)

The Message for Us

It would be a mistake to think that John's words are addressed only to those Christians of the first century who were dabbling with a dangerous heresy long since forgotten. One theologian has said recently that Christians are still liable to catch the Gnostic germ: to view theology as a system of knowledge unrelated to life's experiences and so having no bearing on day to day living. Theology, says John, must be totally centred on a real man of flesh and blood, the truly human Jesus, the Son of God, living still. Theology, says John, must lead to action. 'If a man is rich and sees his brother in need, yet closes his heart against his brother, how can he claim that he has love for God in his heart?' (3:17) One cannot evade such a direct question as this. 'My children! Our love should not be just words and talk; it must be true love, which shows itself in action' (3:18).

THE SECOND AND
THIRD LETTERS OF JOHN

Whereas the First Letter of John was intended for a general audience, these two are addressed to a more clearly defined readership. The 'dear Lady and her children' (1:1) of the Second Letter is probably a pseudonym for one of the churches in Asia Minor. The letter contains an exhortation to charity and a warning against false teachers.

'Gaius, whom I truly love' of the Third Letter (1:1) is in some dispute with Diotrephes, the leader of the church, who pays no attention to John's authority. This letter may be an attempt to replace him.

THE REVELATION TO JOHN

The Background

The author of this book describes himself as 'John, your brother, and in union with Jesus I share with you in suffering . . . I was put on the island named Patmos because I had proclaimed God's word and the truth that Jesus revealed' (1:9). Whether the author of Revelation is to be identified with the author of the Gospel and letters is a matter scholars dispute. The outcome of the dispute (if ever it is settled) does not need to concern us. We know that this is part of the inspired word of God.

The greatest power on earth in the first century after Christ was imperial Rome. Its rule covered most of Europe and Asia Minor. To remain united, this superpower had formulated its own religion—the worship of the Emperor as God. Because Christians refused to worship the Emperor, they were regarded not only as irreligious but as disloyal citizens. It was inevitable that they should suffer a savage persecution. Revelation, written (perhaps in two stages) at the end of the first century AD, is a message of hope to the persecuted. From his vision, John has been given a glimpse of the battle between the forces of evil and the power of God. Victory is already assured. Patience and endurance and hope are the virtues most needed by Christians.

Strange Imagery

The type of writing used by the author is called 'apocalyptic'. (In the older Catholic versions of the New Testament this book was called the Apocalypse.) This sort of literature was common enough at the time of our Lord—and, in fact, is to be found in certain books of the Old Testament. Because it is so foreign to our way of writing and thinking, it presents special difficulties. However, these are not insurmountable, provided we have the key with which to break the code.

It ought to be said straightaway that we will search in vain if we expect to find in Revelation information as to when or how the end of the world will come. This book is not a horoscope.

The strange language, the numbers, the grotesque imagery—these would, for the most part, be intelligible enough to the early Christians. But they would be quite unintelligible to the persecutors. In other words, Revelation is a work from and for the underground Christian.

Keys to the Code

The forces of evil are described in various ways: the red dragon (Satan), beasts (the Emperor deities), the woman dressed in scarlet (imperial Rome), Gog and Magog (devils).

The forces of good: the angel, the Lamb, the warrior, the bridegroom—all these are synonyms for the risen and victorious Jesus. The two women refer to Mary and to the Church, the Bride of Christ.

Numbers are used as symbols. 'Seven' means completeness. (So the seven churches (Chapters 2 and 3) represent the whole Church.)

'Six' is incomplete (that is, it falls short of the perfect 'seven') and so represents evil. The beast's number is six hundred and sixty-six (13:18).

'Twelve' is the number that describes the Church.

'Four' is associated with the earth (the four corners of the earth, 7:1).

These are just a few examples of the symbols used by the author to clothe the message God wanted him to give to his suffering people.

The Message

Jesus lives still and is with his people. He is to be adored as God. God will judge all men, persecutors and persecuted. Those who are faithful to God will be rewarded even though at present they suffer. God alone is supreme. He controls the world and everything in it. Victory over Satan is already won. Nevertheless, Satan can still harass mankind. God's plan for man's salvation is unfolding and inevitably it involves a great battle between the Powers of Light and the Powers of Darkness in the struggle for the salvation of each human being. The hero of this great drama is Jesus himself. At the end God will create a new heaven and a new earth in which God will be at home with men. 'He will live with them, and they shall be his people. God himself will be with them, and he will be their God. He will wipe away all tears from their eyes. There will be no more death, no more grief, crying, or pain. The old things have disappeared' (21 : 3–4).

The Finale

'God will live with them' reminds us of that first idyllic vision of God with men, described in the Old Testament book of Genesis: 'God walking in the garden in the cool of the day' (Genesis 3 : 8). And indeed Revelation contains scores of allusions to other parts of the Bible.

It is as though in this last book of the Bible, John is summing it all up. In doing so, he helps his readers to see at a glance the whole sweep of God's plan for his people, a plan which will reach its climax at the coming of our Lord Jesus. 'So be it. Come, Lord Jesus!' (22 : 20)

BIBLIOGRAPHY

The following books are recommended if the reader wishes to explore the New Testament more deeply:

1 General commentaries and reference books

The New Catholic Commentary on Holy Scripture, ed. R. Fuller & B. Orchard (Nelson, London, 1969)

The Jerome Biblical Commentary (G. Chapman, London, 1969)

The New Bible Commentary Revised (Inter-Varsity Press, London, 1970)

Peake's Commentary on the Bible, revised edition (Nelson, London, 1962)

New Atlas of the Bible, J. H. Negenman (Collins, London, 1969)

Atlas of the New Testament, J. Stirling (G. Philip, London, 1966)

The Bible Readers' Encyclopedia and Concordance, W. M. Clow (Collins, London, 1966)

2 Books about the whole New Testament and its background

Bouquet, A. C., *Everyday Life in New Testament Times* (Batsford, London, 1953)

Davies, W. D., *Invitation to the New Testament* (Darton, Longman and Todd, London, 1967)

Dodd, C. H., *According to the Scriptures* (Nisbet, Welwyn, 1952; Fontana Books, London, 1965)

Lace, O. J., ed., *Understanding the New Testament* (Cambridge University Press, London, 1965)

Neil, W., *The Plain Man Looks at the Bible* (Fontana Books, London, 1965)

Quesnell, Q., *This Good News: Catholic Theology* (G. Chapman, London, 1964)

Rhymer, J., *Bible Lands and People* (G. Chapman, London, 1971)

Ward, M., *They Saw His Glory* (Sheed & Ward, London, 1956)

3 Books about parts of the New Testament

Barclay, W., *The First Three Gospels* (SCM Press, London, 1966)
   The Mind of St Paul (Fontana Books, London, 1966)
Caird, G. B., *The Gospel of St Luke* (Penguin Books, Harmondsworth, 1963)
Dodd, C. H., *The Meaning of Paul for Today* (Fontana Books, London 1958)
Fenton, J. C., *The Gospel of St Matthew* (Penguin Books, Harmondsworth, 1963)
Grossouw, W., *In Christ: Theology of St Paul* (G. Chapman, London, 1962)
Manson, T. W., *Primer of Christianity* (Oxford University Press, London, 1950)
Nineham, D. E., *The Gospel of St Mark* (Penguin Books, Harmondsworth, 1963)
Wansbrough, H., *The Theology of St Paul* (Mercier Press, Cork, Ireland, 1968)

4 Series of books about the New Testament

Bible Study Books—The Scripture Union, London
Layman's Bible Commentaries—SCM Press, London
New Testament Reading Guide—Liturgical Press, Minnesota, USA
Tyndale New Testament Commentaries—Tyndale Press, London
Where We Stand—Darton, Longman and Todd, London

5 Organizations that publish notes and suggestions for people who wish to read a little of the Bible each day

The Bible Reading Fellowship—148, Buckingham Palace Road, London, S.W.1.
The Scripture Union—5, Wigmore Street, London, W.1.

Also available in the Fontana Religious Series

Good News For Modern Man
The New Testament—Today's English Version
Already known to 14 million people this translation has swept
America. Read by all denominations. Combines scrupulous
accuracy with the freshness and urgency of the Christian
message.

Life Line
ALAN WALKER
Alan Walker founded Life Line in Sydney to combat suicide
and help all in need. With its discipline, its efficiency, its
unique round-the-clock telephone counselling and its crash
rescue teams, Life Line shows Christianity in action.

A Woman's Book of Prayers
RITA F. SNOWDEN
'It seems to me to answer almost perfectly to its title. The
language is modern and yet beautiful. I am quite sure that
this book will make prayer more real and meaningful for all
who use it.' *William Barclay*

But That I Can't Believe
JOHN A. T. ROBINSON
Gives the lie to those who say the author of *Honest to God* and
The New Reformation, the man who started the great break-
through in radical theology in Britain, does not speak to the
man in the pew. Warm, lucid explanations of the joys and
doubts of the Christian faith, in down-to-earth language
everyone can understand.

Truth to Tell
HUGH MONTEFIORE
Cambridge sermons which take a pretty sharp look at
Christian faith and Christian ethics today, and suggest
some radical restatements.

Also available in the Fontana Religious Series

Prayers for Help and Healing
WILLIAM BARCLAY
William Barclay's books of prayers have now sold over
400,000 copies in Fontana. Here are prayers to help share
private suffering of mind and body with God.

Letters to a Friend 1950–52
ROSE MACAULAY
Reveals her as one of the great letter-writers of this century.
'The book tingles with wit and blossoms with erudition and
experience.' *Sunday Telegraph*

The General Next to God
RICHARD COLLIER
The story of William Booth, pawnbroker turned preacher,
who founded the Salvation Army in the face of armed mobs,
burned meeting halls and biased courts.

Half-way to Faith
DAVID ECCLES
'Lord Eccles writes with a charm and humility which hold
the reader, and with a perception which should help both
believer and non-believer to be asking the right questions.'
Archbishop of Canterbury, Sunday Times

The Future of Man
TEILHARD DE CHARDIN
A giant footnote on his famous book *The Phenomenon of Man*.
Teilhard here considers the future of mankind at three levels:
science, philosophy and theology. 'It should be read by all
who seek purpose in the universe.' *John Stuart Collis, Sunday
Times*